A Brief History of the Everglades City Area

Marya Repko

ECITY•PUBLISHING

Everglades City, Florida

When I first visited Everglades City in 1990, I was fascinated with the precise town planning and relics of what little I could glean of its history. After I moved here in the winter of 2000, I read everything about the area that I could find in the local library and museum. It seemed there was a need for a small, brief history for visitors and newcomers; something that would quell the curiosity I originally had; more than a guide book but not a scholastic tome.

In this second edition, I resisted the temptation to create a "not so brief" history so I have only made necessary corrections and added some pictures.

My thanks to all my customers for their encouragement and support. Any errors, of course, are mine and I would be glad to hear from readers with comments or suggestions.

Marya Repko
Everglades City
December 2005

A Brief History of the Everglades City Area

© 2001, 2005 text by Marya Repko
All rights reserved.

cover picture from the Storter Collection
courtesy of Collier County Museums, Naples, FL

set in Book Antiqua, 11/14pt
printed and bound in the USA
Second Edition, Third Printing, December 2011

ISBN 978-0-9716006-3-8

ECITY•PUBLISHING

P O Box 5033
Everglades City, FL, 34139
telephone (239) 695-2905
email: ecitypublishing@earthlink.net
website: www.ecity-publishing.com

Other books in this series:

Grandma of the Glades; A Brief Biography of Marjory Stoneman Douglas

Angel of the Swamp; Deaconess Harriet Bedell in the Everglades

A Brief History of the Fakahatchee

A Brief History of Sanibel Island

Historia de Everglades City (translated by Gloria Gutierrez)

Words on the Wilderness;
  A History of Place Names in South Florida's National Parks by Larry Perez

CONTENTS

INTRODUCTION 5
1 SETTLERS 7
   Background History
   Late 1800's
   Turn of the Century
   Early 1900's
   After the 1910 Hurricane
   Arrival of Collier
2 THE TRAIL 23
   Early Developments
   Building the Town
   Building the Road
   Along the Trail
3 THE TOWN 31
   Avenues, Streets, and Buildings
   Other Establishments
   Life in the Town
4 AFTER THE TRAIL 39
   Tomatoes at the Big Farm
   Logging, Ranching, and Fishing
   Moonshine and Bootlegging
   The Park
5 AFTER THE PARK 49
   Mid-Century
   The New City
   Hurricane Donna
   Improvements in the City
6 MODERN TIMES 57
   Around the Area
   In the City
APPENDIX I. CRACKERS 61
APPENDIX II. PLACE NAMES 62
SOURCES 65
INDEX 73

A Brief History of the Everglades City Area

Courtesy of Florida State Archives, Photographic Collection
Southern Florida in a map dating from 1893.

INTRODUCTION

Everglades City, Chokoloskee, and the Ten-Thousand Islands are steeped in history and more than a little mystery and romance. Who could have thought that Potato Creek, a tiny outpost in Florida's "Last Frontier", would one day be a county seat – except, of course, a Tennessee-born advertising mogul with the imposing name of Barron Gift Collier.

Evidence of shell mounds and ancient canals point to the area's occupation in ancient times, probably by the Calusa Indians. More recently, it was a sanctuary for Indians during the Seminole wars. And, it was a refuge for runaway slaves, deserters from the Civil War, and fugitives from the law.

It was a scattering of small hard-working communities who supplied produce from farming, fishing, hunting and forestry to markets north and south.

It had its own ex-pirate, living on his own key, and its own infamous gentleman killer, the subject of historical novels. Later, it was a safe haven for moonshiners and bootleggers, a playground for Al Capone's buddies, and a convenient backwater for smuggling drugs and illegal aliens.

It flourished in the Florida boom as civilization reached south with the completion of the Tamiami Trail and the Atlantic Coast Line railroad, attracting sportsmen for hunting and fishing.

What happened? The Depression crushed the economy; hurricanes discouraged settlers; changes in the Glades eco-system denuded the land of fertility and wildlife; tourists and snow-birds were drawn to the beaches elsewhere in Southwest Florida.

What remains is the old-world elegance of the Rod & Gun Lodge and the legacy of town planning: wide avenues, Circle, and impressive Court House building. History can be found in the Museum (housed in the former laundry), in the Smallwood Store, and in unpreserved relics like Monroe Station along the Trail.

A Brief History of the Everglades City Area

From the Storter Collection, Courtesy of Collier County Museums, Naples, FL
Reverend George Gatewood.

"A good Methodist preacher. Surely he must of been a Christian and had some love. I only remember him as a good man that use to come to Everglade when I was a small boy and what I was told about him. He lived in Punta Gorda but would ride a horse to Naples and borrow a rowboat and row to Everglade to preach. There sure was not much money those days. He must of had something that's lacking these days. I have heard my parents mention him many times and it was always something good. He would leave his horse with Capt. Charlie Stewart in Naples. He also ministered to them. Could you imagine a preacher doing such a thing these days? Yes, if he had a good automobile and a good salary." *For information about the Storter Collection, see page 22.*

1 SETTLERS

Florida was made the 27th State of the Union in 1845 and in 1850 the US Government gave the "swamp and overflowed"[1] land, that now includes Collier County, to the State. As the Indian Wars moved southward, army forts were established on the coasts of southern Florida. For example, Fort Myers (named for General Abraham Charles Myers) was built in 1850 to protect the settlers from the Seminoles led by Billy Bowlegs.

BACKGROUND HISTORY

Many of the settlers were German immigrants, pushing southwards from Georgia, Alabama, and Tennessee in search of better land and a frost-free climate. There were also fugitives: Indians fleeing from the Government's attempt to force them out to reservations in the West, escaped slaves, deserters (called "raiders"[2]) from the Unionist and Confederate Armies, and pirates hiding hostages or burying treasure. When their paths crossed, the slaves and Indians helped each other; the slaves could speak the "white man's" language and the Indians knew how to live off the land.

Some of these refugees found their way to the Everglades, the great "River of Grass" running from Lake Okeechobee southwards, and to the Ten-Thousand Islands, the mangrove keys fringing the southwest coast. Among the settlers, legitimate and otherwise, the same families crop up in the various little communities that were being established. At the turn of the century, names like Weeks, Storter, Brown, House, Hamilton, and

---

[1] Tebeau, *Florida's Last Frontier*, p.13
[2] Beater, *Tales of South Florida and the Ten Thousand Islands*, p.97

Daniels are found throughout the history of this period here and further afield in Marco Island, Naples and Immokalee.

By the late 1800's, there were flourishing settlements on Chokoloskee island and on the Turner River, Halfway Creek, Everglade River, Chatham River, Sand Fly Island and other outposts in the region. Their principle activities were farming, fishing, and hunting. They raised avocados, tomatoes, bananas, pumpkins, citrus fruits and sugar cane. They fished for mullet in the season, dug clams, and harvested oysters. They hunted alligators for hides, raccoons for fur, turtles for meat, birds for plumes. For their own food they killed deer, wild turkeys, and seabirds.

From the Storter Collection, Courtesy of Collier County Museums, Naples, FL
Key West and its busy harbor in the days of sail.

In the early days, Key West was the center of government and commerce. It was the seat of Monroe County (which included the Ten-Thousand Islands) and the terminus of shipping lines to New York and Cuba. Produce for sale went by boat to Key West to be sent onwards and supplies came back from Key West. What mail delivery there was came via Key West. Anyone who was very sick was taken to Key West for medical treatment.

In 1887 Lee County was formed, with the seat in Fort Myers, taking over responsibility for the area from Monroe County. The boundary runs from just south of Chokoloskee island, through Rabbit Key and across the Loop Road. In 1904 the Atlantic Coast Line Railroad reached Fort Myers. Marco Island, under the leadership of W. T. Collier and his son W. D. (Capt. Bill), prospered after clamming became mechanized in 1908. On the east coast, in 1912, Henry Flagler's "Overseas Railway" reached Key West via Miami. Homesteaders began to look north for their trading; new settlers and adventurous tourists made their way further south.

LATE 1800'S

In 1857 during the Third Seminole War, an army contingent of 110 men including Capt. Richard Turner stopped on Chokoloskee island, 144 acres raised by ancient Indian shell mounds. Turner led a party up the nearby river, where they were ambushed by Indians. He came back in 1874, settling near the mouth of the river (where there are also shell mounds) and giving it his name. He also grew tomatoes on Sand Fly Island.

In 1868 William Smith Allen, on the way from his castor bean farm in Sanibel to the business he owned with his brother in Key West, sailed into what is now Everglades City looking for fresh water. He found John Weeks, an army deserter, growing bananas and sugar cane on the river bank. One story is that John had been pressed into the Unionist Army at the outbreak of the Civil War while visiting New York from his parents' home in Virginia; his brother Madison had joined the Confederate Army. Madison found John among the enemy captives after a battle, so they both ran away.

The little river that Allen entered was called Potato Creek because potatoes were growing wild ("volunteering"[3]), planted previously by either the Indians or Civil War soldiers. The name of the river changed several times over the next half-century and was known as the Everglade River, the Allen River, the Storter River, and finally the Barron River. The whole area was referred to as

---

[3] Tebeau, *Florida's Last Frontier*, p.113

A Brief History of the Everglades City Area

Chokoloskee, an approximation of the Indian word for "old home", "old house", or "big house".

In 1870 Allen returned and farmed the east side of the river as far north as what is now the Route 29 bridge. A plume hunter named William Clay also claimed land in the vicinity. Clay sold out to Allen, Weeks moving to Chokoloskee island. Allen built a house on the east bank of the river (on the site of the present Rod & Gun Lodge) which he raised on stilts to a height of six feet after the hurricane of 1873. He was a Justice of the Peace, enabling him to hold court and perform marriages.

Allen was joined in 1879 by Madison Weeks who settled on the west bank of the Allen River, after having stopped briefly at Halfway Creek. Weeks was bought out in 1883 by John Brown, also from Halfway Creek.

In 1881 George Storter, Sr, arrived from Manatee County. Storter and his family had emigrated from Alsace on the French/German border in 1835. He had been adopted by a family in New Orleans and then moved to Alabama. In the 1870's he came south with two sons, after the death of his wife and oldest son, to near Fort Ogden.

Storter initially farmed with Allen, shipping vegetables to Key West. The young Storters, George, Jr, and Robert Bembery (called R.B. or Bembery) joined him in 1882 and helped with the harvesting of cucumbers, eggplant and tomatoes. In the same year, August Swycover, a black man, settled across the river in what was later called Port DuPont and raised sugar cane. The next year, George, Sr, moved north on the river, opposite the Swycover homestead.

In 1887 George, Jr, returned and bought out Swycover. In 1889 he bought out Allen who retired to Key West. George, Jr, paid $800 for all the Allen property and moved into the "house on stilts". His brother Bembery lived nearby, towards the mouth of the river.

On Chokoloskee, Weeks was again bought out, this time by an absentee landlord called Capt. von Pfister who, in turn, was replaced by a Corsican family called Santini. They had helped to free Napoleon and then fled to America to escape retribution. A branch of the family developed the resort of Fort Myers Beach on the barrier island of Estero and one of the modern generation owned the famous dolphin "Flipper" in the Keys.

In 1886 G. C. McKinney, later called the "Sage of Chokoloskee" or the "Daddy of Chokoloskee", arrived from near the Santa Fe River in northern Florida looking for a healthier climate. He initially farmed with Turner and also fished, hunted alligator and chopped wood for $3 per cord. Born in 1847 in Georgia, McKinney's family had moved to Columbia County in 1854. He fought in the Civil War under Captain Hendry around Fort Myers, moonshined, worked on his father's cotton farm, built a water mill with his own hands where he ground corn, added a sawmill that cut lumber for the Plant Railroad, and ran a store with Post Office that he had initiated. As he later wrote "It has always been my plan to believe that I had a head of my own and that it was good for something – not just a knot tied in the top of my backbone to keep it from raveling out"[4].

Meanwhile, other parts of the Ten-Thousand Islands were being occupied. Pavilion Key was home to fur hunters. E. J. Watson, a killer whose story is famous, had found Chatham Bend, to and from which he fled as the law pursued him. Another romantic figure was Juan Gomez, said to have been a pirate, who had settled in the 1870's on Panther Key, also called Goat Key. An attempt to raise goats there ended in failure because the panthers ate them.

In 1882 Joe Wiggins moved his trading post and apiary from Wiggins Pass (on the Imperial River north of Naples) to the Allen River. He also raised cabbages, but left in 1886 for Sand Fly Island.

---

[4] McKinney quoted in Brown, *Totch*, p.253

Halfway Creek was a thriving farming area to which the Reverend George W. Gatewood *(see page 6)* went in 1888 to establish a Methodist chapel. Nearby on the Turner River, a Dr. Harris from Key West established a tomato packing shed, office, stable and cistern.

TURN OF THE CENTURY

By 1890 George Storter, Jr, had enlarged his house on the Allen River and provided rooms for visiting hunters and fishermen. In 1892 he established a store and traded with the Indians. As a leading citizen, he had the first house that was painted in the village of Everglade. Charley Boggess, (who settled at the mouth of the river after living in a number of places around the area) acted as a fishing guide, built boats, and farmed tomatoes on Sand Fly Island.

From the Storter Collection, Courtesy of Collier County Museums, Naples, FL
Storter Store and Trading Post with Seminole Canoes.

George, Sr, had a tin shop on the river bank, over which he lived. He made containers for the syrup that was produced from sugar cane raised by his sons at Halfway Creek and transported from there by barge. George, Jr, boiled down the juice from the cane whereas Bembery evaporated it. The syrup and other produce was taken to Key West on Bembery's schooner "Bertie Lee", which left Everglade every Tuesday and returned on Friday.

From Chokoloskee, McKinney petitioned the Post Office to have regular mail delivery. The authorities dared him to prove that mail could be delivered reliably so he organized trips to and from Key West. In 1891 the Post Office was opened, originally with the name "Comfort" but changed the next year to "Chokoloskee". McKinney was Postmaster and ran a store. The arrival of the mail boat, which was obviously dependent on the weather, was announced with a conch horn.

C. S. (Ted) Smallwood, born in 1873 in Columbia County (near McKinney's sawmill), became to Chokoloskee what the Storter family was to Everglade. In 1883 he moved with his father and uncle to Fort Ogden and in 1891 made his first visit to the Ten-Thousand Islands. For the next five years he did various jobs, traveling to the Keys and Miami. In 1897 he married a local girl, Mamie House, after farming with her father on the Turner River. In 1899 Smallwood bought out Adolphus Santini and rebuilt the house. He farmed and cut buttonwood to make charcoal, another local export, and hunted alligators. Before that, in 1896, he carried the mail to Marco for $1 a day, 3 days a week. On his way, he would stop at Panther Key to see if the old pirate Gomez needed supplies, as did Bembery Storter at various times.

Juan Gomez claimed to have been born in 1778 in either Madeira or the French provinces. He said that he worked on ships and was captured by the possibly mythical pirate Gaspar. In 1805 Gomez fought with Napoleon's army. After more adventures crewing on slave ships, he escaped from pirates to Panther Key in 1821. He helped the Cubans against Spain and was in General Zachery Taylor's command during the Seminole War of 1837. Eventually in 1855, at the alleged age of 77, he returned to Panther Key and built a palmetto dwelling. He lived from hand to mouth, refusing to search for buried pirate treasure, took a wife (reputedly aged 78) in 1884, and died in a fishing incident in 1900. Even his death was mysterious. He either got tangled in his net or got caught up in an overhanging tree; some people claimed that he said he had lived long enough.

From the Storter Collection, Courtesy of Collier County Museums, Naples, FL
Juan Gomez and his wife on Panther Key.

Along the Allen River a Post Office was opened in 1893 with the name "Everglade", suggested by Bembery Storter, although McKinney gives himself credit for helping with the official application. In the same year, the first school teacher, a man named Todd, arrived and taught in a room in George, Jr's, house until the county provided a school near the mouth of the river. Rob Storter, Bembery's son born in 1894, remembers that they never wore shoes to school and only sometimes wore them to church.

Reverend Gatewood moved into a parsonage in Everglade in 1892 and held services in the school. He made friends with the Indians but left after four years because his parishioners had become interested in Adventism. The area was later served by wandering preachers. When the month had five Sundays, the last one was known as "Gomez Sunday" and Bembery took the congregation to hold Methodist services on Panther Key.

McKinney, meanwhile, had been instrumental in getting a school for Chokoloskee. Students were taught intermittently in a palmetto shack but there were advantages to a one-room school.

One student commented much later "You heard everything, so when you got to the next grade you already knew it"[5]. In 1898 Lee County provided the lumber and the residents built the schoolhouse. In the same year, a church was built, McKinney supplying the land and the bell.

However, it was Halfway Creek that was the most important settlement. By 1891 there was an Adventist chapel there. In 1892 the polling headquarters for the first elections in the area were at Halfway Creek. Further down the coast, the House family bought the Turner River property from Dr. Harris in 1895, but moved in 1900 to Chokoloskee after the fields were flooded.

EARLY 1900'S

In 1902 the Shands survey tried to sort out squatters' rights and title transfers to establish who owned land in southwest Florida. The result was that George Storter, Jr, was officially recognized in Everglade and Halfway Creek as was Ted Smallwood and his father in Chokoloskee.

Life continued on a hand-to-mouth basis. As Rob Storter wrote in his reminiscences, they had to "make something out of nothing [because they] never had the something to make anything out of"[6]. Children worked alongside their parents, helping with the fishing and hunting, and made pets of raccoon kittens. Bill Brown and George Storter, Jr, were taking furs to sell in Fort Myers in 1906. George, Jr, operated a sawmill in 1908. The Brown homestead on the opposite side of the river had lush avocado trees and date palms.

Many families set up temporary camps on the keys and river banks to farm or fish or hunt during the season while keeping claim to their homesteads in more settled communities. Clam diggers spent the season on Little Pavilion Key; clams were

---

[5] Hazel Pettit Griffin quoted in Stone, *Dwellers of the Sawgrass and Sand*, vol II, p.426

[6] Storter, *Seventy-seven Years in Everglades, Chokoloskee, Naples*, p.18

plentiful all along the coast, but particularly around Pavilion Key. In 1908 Capt. Bill Collier of Marco invented the clam dredge, putting many of the manual diggers out of work. In 1916-17, red tide hurt the local harvest but the Doxsee cannery in Marco Island operated until 1947. The first ice house for fish was on Sand Fly Rock.

From the Storter Collection, Courtesy of Collier County Museums, Naples, FL s
Clam Diggers' Camp on Little Pavilion Key.

Plume hunting was outlawed in Florida in 1901 but illegal trading continued in this lucrative commodity; at $32 per ounce, feathers were more valuable than gold. The plumes (mostly egret) were used to decorate women's hats. Gregorio Lopez, who had settled on the river bearing his name in 1890, tried to farm birds in Chokoloskee but they ate too much to make it profitable. After the Audubon warden Guy Bradley from Flamingo was shot on Oyster Key in 1905, other states passed legislation and the market gradually disappeared, but not before two more wardens were killed.

On Chokoloskee, Ted Smallwood was appointed Postmaster in 1906 and operated a store where he traded with the Indians, learning their language and gaining their trust. John Weeks piloted the mail boat with a 7.5hp engine three times a week from Chokoloskee and Everglade to Marco. Clothes were ordered from the Sears catalog and ammunition came from Montgomery Ward when not available locally.

McKinney delivered babies (he was a state-registered mid-wife), pulled teeth, and dispensed his accumulated, self-taught medical knowledge when called upon. The traveling dentist would occasionally visit the area with a foot-operated drill.

In Everglade, the next generation of Storters was growing up. In 1907 Neil, son of George, Jr, went to the new Gainesville campus of the University of Florida at age 16. There were only 100 students and he soon got the nickname "Brother Gator", shortened to "Bo Gator", because of his origins in the Glades. His first claim to fame was as the founder of the Bo Gator Club, an excuse for carousing. However, in his final year (1911-12) he took college seriously; he was active in student politics and captained the football team, since known as the "Gators". Neil himself said that the name was coined by a newspaper reporter who wrote about the "Florida Alligators" playing Mercer College, Georgia.

AFTER THE 1910 HURRICANE

From the Storter Collection, Courtesy of Collier County Museums, Naples, FL

The Schoolhouse was washed away by the 1910 hurricane. Note the people on a sugar cane barge to the right.

A hurricane struck in 1910 with consequences throughout the area. The Turner River packing shed was destroyed but the cistern remained and was used by Ted Smallwood. The school in Everglade was washed down the river and later rebuilt. The flooding prompted Ted Smallwood to raise his buildings on stilts after the water receded.

A Brief History of the Everglades City Area

There were dramatic events of a human nature during the storm. E. J. Watson was shot by a posse of local men and/or by the black man Henry Short, said to be defending Grandpa House. In any case, Watson was "good to get along with until he got mad"[7] when he "had to see blood"[8]. He had a substantial house with 13 rooms called Watson Place on Chatham Bend and was a prosperous sugar cane farmer, possibly because he killed his workers rather than paying them. When he arrived at the Smallwood store on the fateful night, he refused to give over his gun and, as some stories tell it, tried to shoot but failed because his ammunition was dampened by the hurricane. Unfortunately, Ted Smallwood said he "did not want anything of it"[9] and remained inside so we do not have his eyewitness report.

After Watson's death, the Brown family lived in Chatham Bend until it was bought by the Chevelier Corporation, a deal arranged by J. F. Jaudon, who tried, and failed, to drain the swamp. There were several reports that the house had blood on the walls.

Another consequence of the hurricane was a Pentecostal revival in Chokoloskee. In 1913 forty people were baptized in the bay. McKinney said he "didn't want all those sins washed up on his yard"[10]. His dry wit and gift of the gab were appreciated in the columns he wrote for the *American Eagle* newspaper for twenty years until his sudden death at age 79 on the dock in the Town of Everglades; he had been picking up supplies after the 1926 hurricane destroyed his store. Fortunately, he had just previously written some "biography and reminiscences"[11] at the request of the paper.

---

[7] Meece Ellis quoted in Stone, *Dwellers of the Sawgrass and Sand*, vol III, p.73

[8] Mary Hamilton Clark quoted in Stone, *Dwellers of the Sawgrass and Sand*, vol III, p.355

[9] Beater, *True Tales of the Florida West Coast*, p.26

[10] Storter, *Crackers in the Glade*, p.55

[11] McKinney quoted in Brown, *Totch*, p.249

A Brief History of the Everglades City Area

Commercial fishing played a big part in the life of the island. Rob Storter and his brother George stayed with their wives in a palmetto shack on Chokoloskee to be near the good fishing. McKinney had commented in 1912 that "Everglade is a small place besides Chokoloskee"[12].

In 1917 Ted Smallwood dredged the channel, moving the fish houses from the bay to either side of his new store (now a museum). He also found fresh water and dug a well. The store was raised up further on stilts after a storm in 1924, enabling it to weather the 1926 hurricane (and all others since).

From the Storter Collection, Courtesy of Collier County Museums, Naples, FL
The "run boat" took ice to the fish house and picked up the catch.

In 1920 Chokoloskee school teachers came and went, finding life among the "swamp angels" (mosquitoes) difficult to endure. Older students took the boat to the high school in Everglades.

In Everglade, the Brown homestead on the west side of the river was divided and half was sold in 1914 to George Bruner, a big game hunter from Indiana. Totch Brown's father operated a tannery, preserving panther and bear skins, but moved temporarily to Fort Myers in 1922.

The first ice plant in Everglade opened in 1922 with Sidney Griffin making deliveries around the town. Sports-fishing became

---

[12] Tebeau, *Story of Chokoloskee Bay Country*, p.18

popular in the area in the early 1920's and provided another source of employment for local fishermen who became guides.

ARRIVAL OF COLLIER

Further afield, Walter Langford of Fort Myers had started planting grapefruit in Deep Lake Hammock, north of Everglade. In 1913 he built a 13-mile railway from there to Port DuPont so that he could carry his fruit to the Allen River for onward shipping.

Courtesy of Florida State Archives, Photographic Collection
The Deep Lake rail cars usually carried grapefruit to the river.

Langford's partner was John Roach who owned streetcars in Chicago. Roach had brought Barron Gift Collier, whose fortune derived from streetcar advertising and other enterprises, to the vacation island of Useppa, supposedly an old pirate hideaway in Pine Island Sound, west of Fort Myers.

Collier "got sand in his shoes"[13]. In 1911 he bought the island with its Inn, made improvements, and promoted the resort for tarpon fishing. Incidentally, gold coins dated 1761 (possibly treasure trove) were found near one of the fairways in 1916 when the golf course was being laid out.

---

[13] Beater, *True Tales of the Florida West Coast*, p.26

A Brief History of the Everglades City Area

Collier was born in 1873 in Memphis, married Juliet Carnes in 1907 and lived mainly in New York. He was attracted to the new challenges of Florida and in 1921 he bought the Deep Lake Hammock citrus farm and railway. He soon owned 900,000 acres in what was to be Collier County.

In 1922 he bought out George Storter, Jr, and in effect owned the village on the renamed Barron River. He also added the "s" to the town name Everglade.

At about this time, a decision had been made to divide Lee County. Barron Collier promised to complete the Tamiami Trail if the division created a county encompassing his lands with the seat in the Town of Everglades. A bill establishing Hendry County to the east and Collier County to the south was passed by the State Legislature in 1923.

Courtesy of Florida State Archives, Photographic Collection
Barron Gift Collier, 1873-1939.

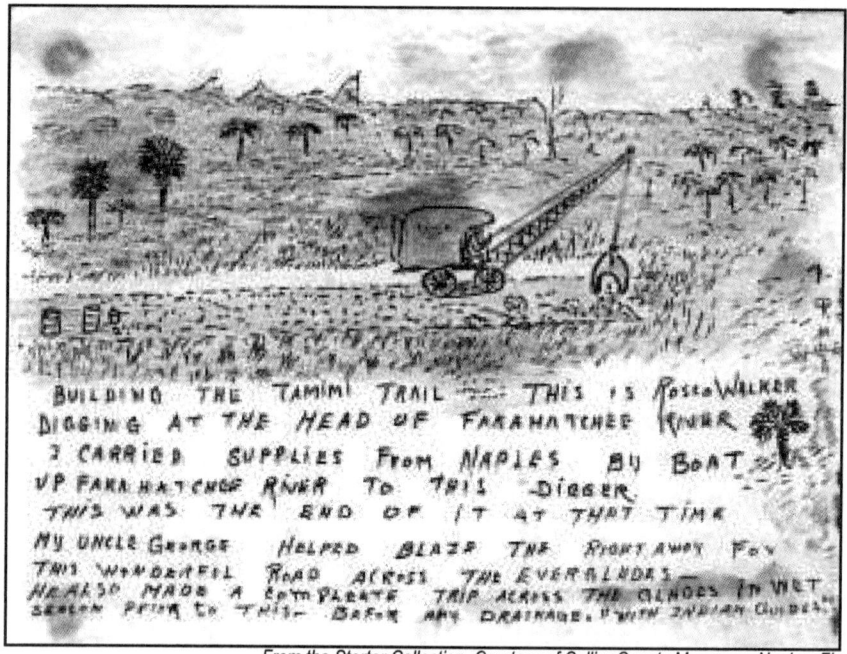

From the Storter Collection, Courtesy of Collier County Museums, Naples, FL

"**Building the Tamiami Trail**" in which Rob Storter tells how he helped bring supplies from Naples by boat to the head of the Fakahatchee River, an area on the Trail about 8 miles west of Route 29. He also writes that "Uncle George helped blaze the right-a-way for this wonderful road across the Everglades -- he also made a complete trip across the Glades in wet season prior to this, before any drainage, 'with Indian guides'".

Rob Storter was the son of R. B. (Bembery) Storter and nephew of George Storter, Jr. Rob was born in Everglades in 1894 and moved to the even-smaller village of Naples in 1916 where he was a commercial fisherman and sports-fishing guide. He observed tremendous changes to the area which he documented in his annotated illustrations. He died in 1987. A collection of more than 300 of his sketches and carved models was acquired by the Friends of the Museum of the Everglades in 2004 and donated to Collier County Museums in 2007.

2 THE TRAIL

The growth of Everglade from rural trading-post village to sophisticated county seat was due to the building of the Tamiami Trail. Described as an undertaking as logistically complex as the construction of the Panama Canal, it required that a self-sufficient support system be built in the middle of swamp country where the only means of transport was by water.

EARLY DEVELOPMENTS

As far back as 1895, Capt. J. F. (Frank) Jaudon, a tax assessor for Dade County, envisioned a loop road around Florida. In 1914-15 he surveyed the route linking Tampa to Miami with the Indian Jack Tigertail and began stirring up interest. There are conflicting stories about the origin of the word "Tamiami", a contraction of Tampa and Miami. It was reportedly proposed by E. P. Dickey at a meeting of the State Roads Department in 1915. Alternatively, it was I. Dixie, President of the Tampa Board of Trade, who coined the name.

Funding was secured in the various Road and Bridge Districts and construction started. The section from Miami to the Dade County line was completed and some work was done on the road south of Naples. This section was important because it linked up with the rail line from the Deep Lake citrus farm. However, the First World War intervened and work stopped. The remainder of the Trail, through mostly uninhabited and uncharted territory, was incomplete.

Even the supposedly completed section was not really finished. The unpaved surface was covered with shells which caused punctures; it took all day to drive from Fort Myers to Naples. In 1921, the naturalist Charles Torrey Simpson described the road

A Brief History of the Everglades City Area

from Naples to Marco Island as "drunk"[1] because it was so rough. He was heading for Deep Lake Hammock to examine local plants and snails. When he got to Marco after his bone-shaking car ride, he took the mail boat to Everglade, then another boat up the river, and finally the rail car, which traveled at 15 mph, north to his destination.

In the same year, J. F. Jaudon and George Storter, Jr, hiked and camped from Everglade to the Dade County line to investigate the feasibility of completing the road. Barron Collier had a strong ally in Mrs. Tommie Barfield of Marco Island, who campaigned with him for the formation of a new county and the completion of the Trail.

In 1923 ten cars, eight of them Model T Fords, carrying 23 white men and 2 Indians, set out from west of Carnestown (the present junction of routes 41 and 29) to drive to the Dade County border. It took eleven days of slogging through mud and hacking through jungle, making repairs to their automobiles en-route and sleeping rough, but the adventurers (called the "Trailblazers") finally reached their destination. Tales of their trip reinforced the need for a road across the Glades.

BUILDING THE TOWN

Collier got busy and hired the best men he could find for his project. David Graham Copeland, born in 1885, attended South Carolina Military Academy and Rensselaer Polytech. He gained engineering experience during World War I working for the Navy. Copeland lived the rest of his life in the Town of Everglades, becoming manager of the Collier Corporation and retiring in 1947. He researched the history of the area but died in 1949 before he was able to turn his studies into a book.

The river was dredged to provide a deeper channel for shipping and to fill in the land on which the new town was to be

---

[1] Rothra, *Florida's Pioneer Naturalist*, p.152

constructed. When more landfill was needed, the area to the east (now known as Lake Placid) was dredged. One of the mechanical dredges was named "Barcarmil" after Collier's three sons Barron, Jr, Carnes and Miles.

A town center was built with all the facilities needed for a productive and comfortable life-style: site offices, bank, laundry, barbershop, drugstore, general merchandise emporium, grocery, bakery, hospital, school, church, and hotel with restaurant. There was even a parking garage for private cars.

Heavy industrial activity took place at the community in Port DuPont, across the river to the north of the town. There was a machine shop for repairing equipment, foundry, shipyard, sawmill to prepare lumber for bridges and buildings, boatyard, and housing for black workers with canteen, recreation hall, pool room and bowling alley, church and school.

A battery-powered streetcar, the only one south of Tampa, connected the north end of the town with the center. No fare was charged and children rode it to school. Obviously, Barron Collier ensured that the car was complete with advertising.

A work camp and warehouse was built at Carnestown, the crossroads named after Collier's wife and one of his sons. A canal and road from DuPont to Carnestown linked the engineering center to work-in-progress. The old Deep Lake railway was used to bring logs to the sawmill at DuPont; other supplies came by ship up the river.

Collier had also committed to providing a road (now Route 29) between the Trail and Immokalee, so a smaller version of the engineering facilities in DuPont was replicated in Carnestown. Near this road, he rebuilt the old Deep Lake railway which became part of the Atlantic Coast Line, a possible rival route to Key West. The railway terminated at the Depot (now a restaurant) in the Town of Everglades.

A Brief History of the Everglades City Area

A full team of surveyors and map-makers was employed at the headquarters in Everglades. As an example of Copeland's inventiveness and thoroughness, he used aerial photography to help in the difficult task of charting the Glades. An aerial survey was also made in 1928 to establish the Collier/Monroe county border.

BUILDING THE ROAD

The roadbed was raised up above flood level by dredging out a channel alongside and using the dug up material as landfill. The resulting waterway is called a "borrow canal" because the engineers "borrow land to build the road"[2]. Most of the dredges were built in DuPont and, in total, 11 of them were maintained there. The Bay City Walking Dredge, operated on the Trail by Meece Ellis and Earl Ivey, can now be seen in Collier Seminole State Park (just south of the corner of Routes 41 and 92).

To service workers on the Trail itself, mobile camps provided bunks and food as well as engineering tools for minor repairs. These primitive trailers were built in DuPont. Some were on wheels, others floated on the canal dug out parallel to the Trail. There were even portable toilets, barrels with the tops and bottoms cut off. Some of the dredges also had living quarters. Telephone lines advanced along with the Trail to keep men at the front line in touch with the office in the Town of Everglades.

As work progressed eastwards, the dredges hit limestone. The rest of the way, some 31 miles, had to be blasted out with over 2.5 million sticks of dynamite, brought by ship up the river to DuPont, then to Carnestown and by oxen down the Trail.

Conditions for workers were terrible, despite the good food and lodging provided by the trailers and the good pay of $60/month. Much of the time the men stood in swamp, covered with mosquitoes. A clinic in the Town of Everglades was set up to treat

---

[2] McIver, *True Tales of the Everglades*, p.23

"muck poison" on the feet of Trail laborers. It was said that there were three crews, many from south Georgia: one on the way down from recruitment in Tampa, one working on site, and one on the way back to Tampa to look for other jobs.

Courtesy of Florida State Archives, Photographic Collection
Dredges working on the Tamiami Trail.

In 1926 the State took over responsibility for the Trail after raising money with Collier's backing. Personnel from the Roads Department arrived in the Town of Everglades to manage the project. Labor was more plentiful because the Florida land boom had collapsed after the hurricane of that year.

In anticipation of the completion of the Trail, Collier started a bus line in 1923, called the Tamiami Trail Tour Bus Line, to carry freight as well as passengers. Initially, it only went from Tampa to Ft Myers but then was extended to Marco Island where passengers could board a boat for the Town of Everglades. When the Trail was finished, the bus line went all the way to Miami. Indians rode free, in gratitude for their help in surveying the route. The line was renamed Trailways and eventually sold by the Collier company.

A Brief History of the Everglades City Area

Courtesy of Florida State Archives, Photographic Collection
Barron Collier (center) greeting visitors at the formal opening of the Tamiami Trail in Everglades, 1928.

April 26th, 1928, was the day of the official opening of the Trail. A convoy of 500 cars, carrying Barron Collier and other luminaries, set out from Ft Myers at 8:30 in the morning, reaching the Town of Everglades at 11:10 a.m. where ceremonies and refreshments were enjoyed. The motorcade then proceeded to the stone archway at the Dade County line and then to Miami. A vehicle from the Tour Bus Line also made the trip, stopping at Everglades (the train did not carry passengers until June of that year). The town was the center of attention, with attractions for the crowds at the Collier County Fair and Tamiami Exposition.

ALONG THE TRAIL

Although the Trail was officially finished, work continued on the Loop Road, which runs south from Monroe Station. It led to the settlement of Pine Crest on Route 94, a prosperous cypress logging community in the 1920's and later a favored hunting area and swamp buggy playground for visitors from Miami. In 1928 a sub-division was created in the area by J. F. Jaudon. The Gator Hook Bar served local residents and visitors.

A Brief History of the Everglades City Area

Along the Trail, Collier established the Southwest Mounted Patrol to aid travelers. The six stations, about ten miles apart, were each occupied by a family. The husband (dressed in red tunic, black pants and hat in the style of the Canadian Mounties) drove up and down the Trail on a motorbike. His aim was to help stranded vehicles. The only reason he carried a gun was to shoot panthers and black bears. The Sheriff from the Town of Everglades was called whenever law enforcement was needed.

The wife stayed at the station where she sold gas and simple food such as soda and sandwiches. The husband was paid $100 per month, the wife $50. Gas cost $1.00 for 5 gallons, oil was 15 cents a quart, soda was 5 cents. All the revenue went directly to Manhattan Mercantile, Collier's retail enterprise, and was collected every week.

Life at the stations could be difficult. Although there was a telephone, the station had to generate its own electricity. The Mounties hunted deer and turkey to eat; the deer took refuge on the high road surface during tropical storms. One of the wives described how scary it was to cope with the isolation of Monroe Station over night with small children when her husband had been detained in the Town of Everglades.

The stations were, from west to east, Belle Meade, Royal Palm Hammock (Routes 41 & 92), Weaver's Camp (correction camp near the mouth of the Fakahatchee River), Turner River (near Ochopee), Monroe Station (now an abandoned restaurant), and Paolita (named for Copeland's daughter) on the Dade border. During the Depression, the Mounties were disbanded and in 1932 the State Police took responsibility for patrolling the Trail.

At Royal Palm Hammock, Collier had set aside some 6,500 acres for the benefit of all citizens to enjoy the Florida landscape as it was in early times. The park, now Collier Seminole State Park, had two large pillars at the entrance and served as a county museum in the 1920's and 30's. It was established as a State Park after World War II. Today the park has a camp site, boat tour, gift shop, a monument to Barron Collier and an original Trail dredge. Each year in February it hosts a Bluegrass Festival ("Jammin' in the Hammock") which includes local crafts booths and interesting food vendors.

Courtesy of Collier County Museums, Naples, FL

Aerial view looking east down Broadway in the Town of Everglades in 1928. The Post Office building with tower is at the bottom left of picture and the Bank is in the triangle. On the right are the Inn, Community Center, garage and laundry. The County Court House is on the north-east quadrant of Circle and the railroad depot is at the eastern end of Broadway on Lake Placid.

3 THE TOWN

Copeland was instructed to lay out a town for a projected population of 5000. The aim was to create an environment that would have a high-enough standard of living to keep staff. Collier provided a home for everyone who worked for him. Houses were built in a variety of styles to avoid the appearance of barracks. Every detail was thought of, including the color of the paint and roof tiles.

The town was attractive with tree planting and other landscaping, such as the goldfish pond in the center of the main thoroughfare. According to one resident, "the Colliers kept Everglades very clean, with flowers on the corners"[1]. Ed Black, dressed in his Collier uniform, raised and lowered the flag every day and swept the streets. The Town of Everglades was a "lovely little oasis nestled in the sawgrass swamp, mosquitoes and all"[2].

AVENUES, STREETS, AND BUILDINGS

Copeland made the center of the town the Circle with the main street, Broadway, running east and west on either side. Copeland Avenue ran north and south from the Circle so that the town was essentially divided into quadrants. Avenues ran north to south, streets were parallel to Broadway, east to west. Riverside Drive curved along the river bank, eventually leading to Chokoloskee Drive which was laid out to follow the Bay. In a 1931 map, an area labeled "golf course (under construction)" is shown at the mouth of the river.

---

[1] June Jolley Dyches quoted in Carlin, *I Remember Marco*, p.71
[2] Merle Surrency Harris quoted in Stone, *Dwellers of the Sawgrass and Sand*, p.458

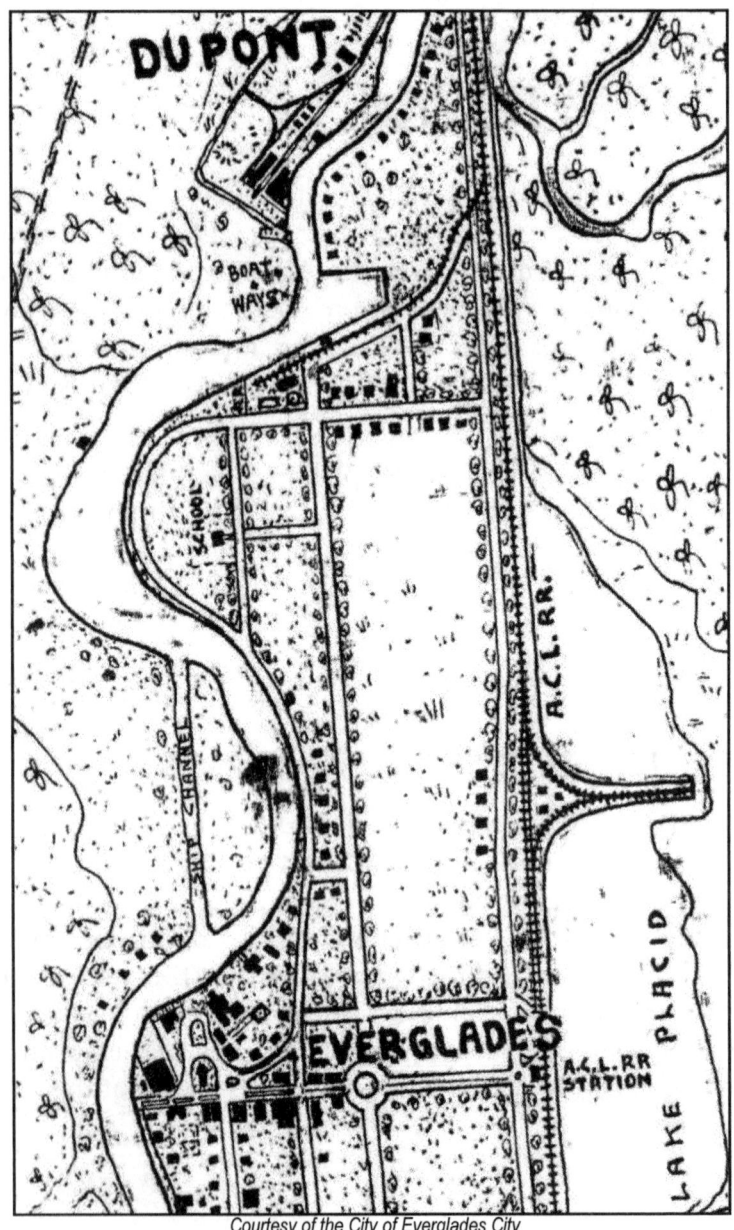
Courtesy of the City of Everglades City
Everglades in 1926, from an aerial photograph.

A Brief History of the Everglades City Area

Many of the street names honored people of the time: Copeland Avenue, Collier Avenue, Barron, Carnes and Miles streets for Collier's three sons, Nebiker and McGee streets for two mapmakers working for Collier, Buckner was a friend of Collier. A map dated 1926 shows how much progress had been made in a few years; the major streets exist, flanked by buildings in clusters at either end of the town. The ACL Rail Road and station are present.

The "business district" was at the west end of Broadway, near the Rod & Gun Club. The administration building was the nerve center of operations. It also housed the telegraph office. Next to it was the Post Office, with the telephone exchange on the second floor and, after 1926, the State Roads Department office. The weather station was on top of the Post Office building and gave the highest view of the city. Storm flags were flown from a pole at the pinnacle. There was also a warehouse on the river bank and a store house in which engineering papers and supplies were kept.

The end of the trolley track was at the river bank on Broadway. The streetcar suffered a fire in 1928 when the batteries were being charged but kept running until a storm in 1929 washed out the track. Electricity, generated by the Railway Light and Power Company, was provided throughout the city.

The Everglades Inn was constructed on the south side of Broadway in 1924. Originally it was only two storeys, used for temporary accommodation until staff had a home built. The third floor was added in 1928 for guests and at its apogee the Inn had 45 rooms. On the ground floor, there was a lounge and dining room presided over by Claus ("Snooky") Senghaas, a chef Collier had discovered in southern Germany during one of his European trips. There was also a drug store operated by Walter Holzman and an outlet of the Manhattan Mercantile department store, another Collier enterprise. Branches of the store operated in DuPont, Collier City (on Marco Island), Immokalee, and Fort Myers. The warehouse was in DuPont.

A Brief History of the Everglades City Area

Courtesy of Florida State Archives, Photographic Collection
The Everglades Inn, social center of the town.

Next door to the Inn on the corner of Allen Avenue was the Community Center (Everglades Club), where movies were shown on Saturday nights and church services held on Sundays. Further east on Broadway was the bakery, barbershop, a large parking garage and the laundry. The bus station was across from the Inn.

Although the laundry building was owned by the Collier company, Chris and Lois Ayers bought the equipment and ran the business with the help of Lois's brother Ralph Echols. They washed the linens for the Inn and Rod & Gun Club as well as providing personal service for local residents. Even Barron Collier had his laundry done there and would send it by mail boat from Useppa when he was staying at that resort. The employees, many of them relatives, slept on cots and Lois cooked for them all. The laundry closed during the Second World War when workers were difficult to hire.

On the north side of Broadway was the grocery and market. The Bank was built next to that in 1927, having previously had temporary offices in several buildings in the town since its establishment in 1923. The library was across from the laundry.

The Court House on the Circle was not ready until 1928. Before that, the county court met in the Rod & Gun Club, the Manhattan Mercantile office, or the old Bank building. Diagonally across the Circle was the jail, with an apartment over it for the Chief of Police. The sheriff lived in a building behind the Inn.

OTHER ESTABLISHMENTS

The Inn and the Rod & Gun Club were not the only places to stay. Bembery Storter's Seminole Lodge was on Riverside Drive South and there were several buildings with apartments. The recreation hall in DuPont was moved in 1925 to the north end of Buckner Avenue where it served as a mess hall. It eventually became a boarding house operated by Earl and Agnes Ivey who charged guests $15 per week.

The Juliet Carnes Collier Hospital, on the river north of the Rod & Gun, was completed in 1929. It had five rooms for patients, a full-time resident doctor and two nurses. Collier provided specialist treatment in Miami when local facilities were not sufficient.

The school, which had been moved further up the river to its present site, was enlarged in 1923 to two rooms and had 45 pupils. It expanded further in 1926 and catered for students from grades 1 through 12. Basketball was the major sport for both girls and boys.

A church and school for blacks were built in 1927 in DuPont. One Everglades teacher said that the DuPont school was nicer than the one in the town for whites. Black students were bussed to high school in Immokalee.

DuPont had a major fire and was re-built with less haste and more care in 1928. The garage serviced motorbikes for the Mounties and in the 1930's an adjacent warehouse held Collier's large collection of antique cars and railroad engines.

A Presbyterian congregation was established in 1925 and met in the Community Center. The church on the Circle was not built until the late 1930's on land donated by Collier and was dedicated as the Community Church in 1940.

In 1933 Deaconess Harriet Bedell came to the town and revived the Glade Cross Mission (idle after its founding near Immokalee in 1898) in a house subsidized by the Collier Development company. Born in 1875, the Deaconess taught in her native Buffalo, N.Y., before going to a mission for the Cheyenne in Oklahoma and then on to the Eskimos in Alaska. It was on a fundraising trip to Miami that she decided the Florida Seminoles needed her services.

Courtesy of Florida State Archives, Photographic Collection
Deaconess Harriet Bedell.

From her new home in the Town of Everglades, she traveled throughout the area, encouraging the Indians to let her sell their crafts to retailers, some of them as far away as New York. She would not take any profit for herself and relied on contributions to keep the Mission active; for example, Collier donated the food for her annual Christmas party for the Indians. She was generally well-liked by all races and well-known throughout the area. She taught Sunday School and sewing in Marco Island and was welcome during hurricanes to take refuge with the Gaunts in Ochopee.

LIFE IN THE TOWN

Collier essentially owned everything in the Town of Everglades, except for the fisheries and the Atlantic Coast Line Rail Road. There was even a dairy farm at the mouth of the river with a bull named "Barron". The cows drowned in a hurricane and the farm was closed.

Everglades was a company town. A whistle blew at various times throughout the day: to wake everyone up and to signal the start of work, lunch break, and the end of the working day. At Christmas, Copeland put up a tree and gave out turkeys and hams.

Wages were paid in a combination of cash and scrip, notes that could only be spent in the Collier establishments. If you had cash, Smallwood's store on Chokoloskee was cheaper. Some employees were furnished with khaki uniforms which were washed, ironed, and repaired free of charge at the laundry.

The Town of Everglades was the civilized center for the area. Boys from Chokoloskee arrived by boat to eat ice cream or drink beer. On Sundays there were snake fights (cock fighting was illegal) in front of the Court House; spectators sat on the steps and bet among themselves. The prisoners entertained by singing at the Community Center, where there were also dances and sing-alongs on different nights of the week. The Indians came to the movies on Saturdays. On the Fourth of July there was a greased pole to climb for a prize pig, a watermelon-eating contest with participants' hands tied behind their backs, and a tug-of-war between the town and Chokoloskee.

The Town of Everglades was "a big social whirl"[3]. There were meetings of the Women's Club, the Auxiliary, and the Lions (who gathered at the Rod & Gun). The Masons' Lodge, the first in Collier County, had been founded in 1927.

---

[3] James Gaunt quoted in Stone, *Ochopee*, p.47

A Brief History of the Everglades City Area

The Inn was "the hub of all social life"[4] and Snooky Senghaas was idolized for the meals he turned out. Less formal fare was provided at the Drug Store (later Mama Dot's Malt Shop, where the hamburgers were renowned) and in the Junglette Café (later the Tropical Café) across from the laundry. The Rod & Gun was refurbished and reopened under Snooky's management in 1925. It was headquarters for some 40 charter boats operated by local fishing guides.

Distinguished visitors were drawn to the Town. Zane Grey came for the fishing in the 1930's. Poet Robert Frost lunched during a visit from his winter home in Coconut Grove. Ted Williams fished and played baseball with kids at the school. Richard Nixon fell off the boat he had chartered. Ike and Mamie Eisenhower praised the Rod & Gun, which kept up its high standards under Snooky, who died in 1954.

Courtesy of Florida State Archives, Photographic Collection
Rod & Gun Club from the Barron River with hospital houses on left.

---

[4] "Everglades Greatest Day" by Frank F Tenney, Jr, in Hoffman, Henry R, ed., *Collier County Heritage*, p.46

4 AFTER THE TRAIL

The presence of the Trail helped to ameliorate the ravages of the harsh economic climate of the late 1920's and 1930's. The Florida land boom had collapsed after the hurricane of 1926, which scared away tourists and potential settlers. The Depression following the fall of the Wall Street markets in 1929 further reduced development.

However, food is always in demand, albeit at a lower price, and the area around Everglades was mostly involved in farming and fishing.

TOMATOES AT THE BIG FARM

In 1928, James Gaunt and his father bought 250 acres on the Trail east of Carnestown from J. F. Jaudon. They paid $100 per acre for the initial parcel and soon bought more. They went into business with J. B. Janes, a man with local interests, and established that the land south of the Trail was too salty but the soil north of the road was suitable for growing tomatoes.

Gaunt called his new venture Ochopee, a misspelling of the Indian word "Ochoppee" meaning "big farm" or "big field". His first task was to build housing for the workers he would have to employ. Most of these were blacks; the ones from Georgia lived in an encampment called Boardwalk because a wooden walkway had to be built over swampy ground to reach it. Gaunt lived with his sister and brother-in-law Ralph Brown who ran the store.

At the same time, he built a packing house for his produce. A mile and a half from Ochopee, H. W. Bird and J. F. Jaudon also built a packing house which they called Birdon, a contraction of their last names and now the name of a road in the area.

Fertilizer was transported on the railroad from Immokalee. The mules that pulled the fertilizer spreaders had to wear leather shoes to prevent them from sinking into the ground. Only men worked in the fields; the women and children carried water to them. Gaunt even used the shoulders of the road, where the ground was too high to be flooded, and planted what he thought were the longest tomato rows in the county along the Trail.

Courtesy of Florida State Archives, Photographic Collection
Indians helped with tomato-picking in Ochopee.

In 1930 Gaunt married and built a home in the white enclave. By this time, there were 250 people in the thriving little town which had a boarding house, restaurant, garage and filling station, and its own electricity plant. In 1932 it was granted a Post Office which operated from the general store. By 1937 Ochopee was described as "almost as big as Naples"[1].

The spirit of paternalism was obvious here, as it was in the enterprises controlled by Barron Collier. Gaunt was described as a "good man to work for"[2], "one of the nicest people you would ever know"[3], and Ochopee was a "fine place to live in"[4]. There

---

[1] Harley Chesser quoted in Stone, *Dwellers of the Sawgrass and Sand, vol III*, p.123
[2] Lilly Belle Warren in Stone, *We Also Came*, p.203
[3] Merle Surrency Harris in Stone, *Dwellers of the Sawgrass and Sand, vol II*, p.470
[4] Lilly Belle Warren in Stone, *We Also Came*, p.203

were landscapers to keep the living quarters tidy and regular garbage collection. The town was provided with its own black church; whites went by bus to the church and school in the Town of Everglades.

As Gaunt said in an interview before he died, "Settlers in the area were non-conformists. They wanted to live their own lives and didn't want anyone to tell them what to do. They wanted to create their own world."[5]

Nearby in Copeland, three Janes brothers (J. B., Winford and Wayne) and their brother-in-law Alfred Webb had also started growing tomatoes in 1930. A commissary and a restaurant were built. Workers were paid in special coinage stamped with a "J".

They were still farming during the war, when labor was scarce and Indian women picked the crop. In the 1940's tomatoes were picked green, sorted, dipped in hot wax, wrapped in tissue and packed in flat boxes. The pay for conveyor belt workers was $0.85/hour.

In Deep Lake, one of Collier's companies operated a canning plant and had as many as 50 black workers picking fruit. Avocados were exported to Key West from Chokoloskee until the hurricane of 1926. Bee-keeping was popular; there were hives around the Town of Everglades and Copeland. The honey was brought to Marco in the 1940's. Dan House farmed tomatoes in 1934-35 on the prairie named after him near Port of the Islands.

LOGGING, RANCHING, AND FISHING

The lumber business became viable after the Trail was completed. In the 1930's there were small mills and logging camps throughout the area. Individual post cutters, living primitively in shacks in the woods, chopped up dead pine trees in Fakahatchee

---

[5] James Gaunt in Stone, *Ochopee*, p.59

Strand and sold them in 8-foot lengths for 25 cents each to ranchers in Immokalee.

The Lee Tidewater Cypress Company, which owned 100,000 acres in 1913, started cutting down the trees in the Big Cypress Swamp in the 1940's. The little community of Lee Cypress (near Copeland) had sturdy houses built of cypress for 29 white and 50 black families; 200 men including Indians (who lived in their own camps) traveled as far as 40 miles on the slow logging train to the edge of the cypress. Trees were cut down with double-handed saws, with an extra man in attendance just to keep away the horseflies.

Courtesy of Florida State Archives, Photographic Collection
Pine and Cypress were logged extensively.

A local resident known throughout the County was Anna Mae Perry, a midwife whose husband worked at the logging operation in the 1940's. "Mother" Perry was welcomed to deliver babies of all races (white, black, Hispanic) except Indian. She also organized a bus to take high school students to Immokalee because the nearby black school only went up to the 8th grade.

Further north on Route 29 at Jerome, the C. J. Jones Company (which previously had a sawmill in Naples on what is now 10th

A Brief History of the Everglades City Area

Avenue) cut pine from 1940 until 1956 when the woods were depleted. After the operation was closed, the sawmill burnt down and most of the housing was moved.

On the prairies north of the Trail and east of Naples, cattle ranching was prosperous and cattle rustling was prevalent. There were few enclosed fields and cattle ran wild, even within living memory. After World War II cattle were fenced in around Miles City (Route 29 and I75) where Collier had stored a big dredge in the early 1930's and had operated a tomato packing house. Cattle in sugar cane country were fed molasses to make them thirstier and help in weight gain.

However, the opening of the Trail was not beneficial to everyone. The fish houses in Chokoloskee moved to the Town of Everglades after 1928 to be closer to transport. The price of fish dropped so low in the area during the Depression that in 1934 local fishermen organized a union (with dues of $1.50 per month) to force wholesalers to pay them more. High school students in the Town of Everglades were given time off when the mullet were running.

Life was difficult. Totch Brown describes how his family moved to Possum Key, set up camp and lived off the land and water. By the time he was a teenager, although he had no "school learning", he was proficient in farming, hunting, fishing and survival. Christmas dinner was "Chokoloskee chicken", the curlew (ibis, a wading bird). The basic diet consisted of white bacon, grits and biscuits supplemented by game, fish, and swamp cabbage.

MOONSHINE AND BOOTLEGGING

One characteristic of the Ten-Thousand Islands was that the area was almost beyond the reach of the law. Florida has been described as "bounded on the North by the Supreme Court and on the other sides by the three-mile limit"[6]. Even before Prohibition, moonshine was made and sold to the Indians. During

---

[6] Beater, *Tales of South Florida and the Ten Thousand Islands*, p.144

A Brief History of the Everglades City Area

the 1890's, the plume hunting era, Frank Wilkerson had a still, thought to be somewhere east of Monroe Station at the end of Lostman's (Lossman's) River. He would take his whiskey by boat via the canoe trails through the Glades to the Storter trading post in Everglade.

Courtesy of Florida State Archives, Photographic Collection
Moonshine was a thriving business.

The Prohibition Amendment became effective at the beginning of 1920 (and was repealed in 1933). By 1923, Chokoloskee had a booming industry in what was called "white mule" or "jugged lightning" or "low bush lightning". Finer drink, such as brandy and Scotch, was brought from the Bahamas and rum came from Cuba. The pass to Chokoloskee was dynamited so that the bootleggers would not have to wait for the high tide. In the Town of Everglades, the boats snuck up the Barron River after lights-out at midnight. Cases of drink were hidden among the crates of carrots or tomatoes on the boxcars going to market for onward shipment to the big cities.

A Brief History of the Everglades City Area

In 1924 in Naples "you couldn't buy a loaf of bread but you could buy liquor at five different places"[7]. One bootlegger, operating privately, got whiskey from Nassau and told a potential purchaser to "give me the money and I'll tell you where it is hidden"[8]. The secret places could be in little watery coves or even under a church. This was confirmed by Earl L Baum, a retired doctor and local historian living in Naples, who was sent on a devious route from Marco Island up a creek in a skiff to a dock and then by boat to Chokoloskee.

During the 1930's the Sheriff would send the Chief of Police out of town when the bootleggers wanted to land their haul. Unfortunately, Chief Bill Hutto was in town on Christmas Eve of 1931 and was shot dead in the course of making an arrest.

Smuggling was not confined to drink. Around the same time illegal aliens (mostly Chinese), found their way to new lives in America via the Ten-Thousand Islands. After World War II, before the land was cleared for cane farming, sugar was smuggled from Cuba to become one of the ingredients for potent drink.

More recently, "pot hauling" (the smuggling of marijuana) was prevalent. Totch Brown candidly describes some of his escapades in the late 1970's and 1980's, such as running out 150 miles in the Gulf to a mother ship and disguising his haul, appropriately, under crab pots. Light aircraft were also used to deliver dubious merchandise.

Given the proximity to Miami, it is not surprising that organized crime was involved in the area. Dutch Schultz of the Chicago Purple Gang is said to have had an interest in Pine Crest. That part of the Loop Road was described as "lawless" because it was over the border in Monroe County, administered from Key West. Al Capone was known to operate a club there where his cronies could enjoy girls and gambling. It burnt down around 1928. Even

---

[7] Bob Combs quoted in Stone, *Dwellers of the Sawgrass and Sand, vol III*, p.45

[8] Alto Griffin quoted in Stone, *The Tamiami Trail*, p.40

with Capone in jail, there was mob presence in the area; his young son was in a big car that stopped at the garage in Ochopee. The driver/bodyguard asked the station owner not to say anything because the boy thought his father was "off somewhere"[9], implying he was off on business.

THE PARK

In 1947 the Everglades National Park, including land donated by the Collier company, was opened by President Harry S Truman. Part of the ceremony was held in the Town of Everglades, thanks to the efforts of Miles Collier. Deaconess Bedell gave the invocation and had lunch with the President at the Rod & Gun Club.

Courtesy of Florida State Archives, Photographic Collection

President Truman in 1947 at the formal ceremonies in Everglades for the opening of the Everglades National Park

However, for local families, the takeover of "their territory" by the government was a disaster. No longer could they fish the waters in Florida Bay and along the coast to Chokoloskee. Cape Sable, once a market garden, was closed to farming. Flamingo, a thriving village occupied by professional fishermen and hunters, became a

---

[9] Hazel Pettit Griffin quoted in Stone, *Dwellers of the Sawgrass and Sand*, vol II, p.449

A Brief History of the Everglades City Area

campground and tourist center. The "tincanners" (tourists with their tin trailers, tin boats and tins of food) were resented.

Most of Pine Crest and the Loop Road became part of the Park. In 1950 a group of eight hunters, based at camps near Monroe Station, formed the Everglades Conservation and Sportsmen's Club to help the state stop illegal and abusive hunting. The area had become popular for weekenders with swamp buggys from the big east coast cities who had no respect for the Glades. The Club organized the first Wild Hog Barbeque (which is still held every year in the late winter) to raise money for their cause. The Pine Crest Lodge and Glader Park trailer resort served sportsmen. In 1952 the Air Boat Association was formed by ten "swamp rats" to protest about the restriction on frog and wild hog hunting.

As Gaunt predicted as far back as 1930, the draining of the Glades eventually ruined the land. Although the Caloosahatchee River was dredged in the 1880's, the program was really started in earnest in 1906 by Napoleon Bonaparte Broward, Governor of Florida. A 75-mile long canal was built from Ft Lauderdale to Lake Okeechobee. The first "overland" voyage by steam ship from Gulf to Atlantic, via the Caloosahatchee and the new waterway, was made in 1912. Broward was honored for his endeavors when a new county, named after him, was carved out of Dade and Palm Beach counties in 1915.

These and other canals stopped the annual floods, which had made the farm land so fertile, and allowed salt water to seep into once-sweet soil. The land boom, encouraged by the promise of new agricultural land, turned into disappointment as crops failed.

In undeveloped areas, drainage changed the vegetation which, in turn, drove away the wildlife. The deer were deliberately killed in 1948. A plague of cattle tick prompted a mass killing of all wild cattle and deer. During the Tick Eradication Scheme, the state paid hunters $80/month, plus supplies, to kill all the deer they could by whatever means, including "firehunting" (jack lighting). Sportsmen protested that other wild animals besides deer, such as raccoon, could spread ticks. The scheme was eventually stopped in the early 1950's after the Indians forced the issue by refusing to let bounty hunters onto their reservations.

The land was further depleted as it was denuded of trees. The royal palms were cut down or transplanted to gardens in the new cities. The pines on the prairies were cut down and the land burnt off by the cattlemen. The cypress were cut down for lumber. The result was a desolate landscape.

In 1968 the area was threatened by the development of the Everglades Jetport, a proposal put forward by Dade County for a second Miami airport. After much bitter wrangling between conservationists (including sportsmen) and business interests, the plan was abandoned. Marjory Stoneman Douglas, whose 1947 book *The Everglades: River of Grass* was so influential, founded the Friends of the Everglades at this time.

It remains to be seen if the Everglades Restoration program can reverse some of the damage.

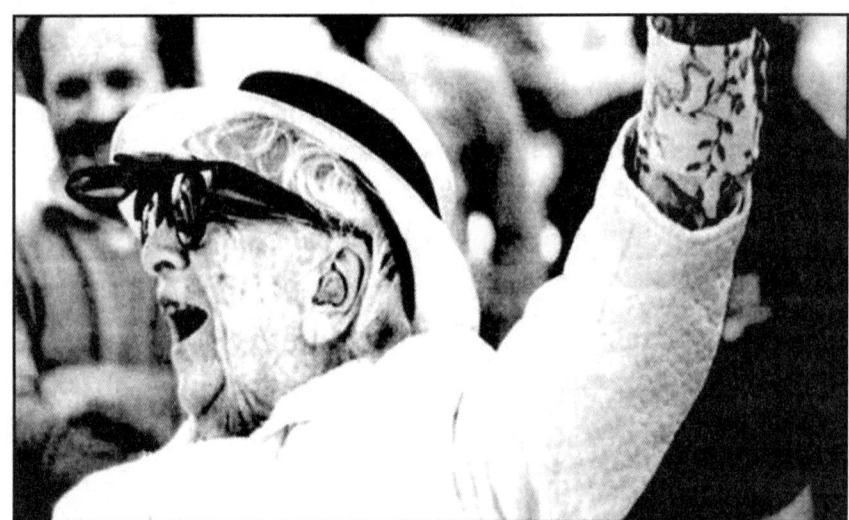

Courtesy of Florida State Archives, Photographic Collection

Marjory Stoneman Douglas (1890-1998) saw many changes in Florida during her long life and believed that "water is the key" to the health of the Everglades.

5 AFTER THE PARK

The 1950's were a decade of change in the area and the 1960's saw large-scale development (some by the Collier Corporation) further afield in Marco Island and Naples, drawing away much-needed industry.

MID-CENTURY

In 1953 Ochopee, with 180 registered voters and a population of over 200, had a catastrophic fire. It started in the boarding house room of a passing visitor (who died because he rushed back to get his clothes in a fit of modesty). The fire destroyed the store and Post Office but farm records were saved.

A shed used for storing hoses and pipes was moved to the roadside as a temporary Post Office and bus stop ticket outlet. In 1960 mail delivery began from the little make-shift Post Office. The route's 123 miles covers Copeland, Jerome, Birdon, the Loop Road and families along the Trail.

After the fire, Gaunt closed the packing shed and living quarters. Workers were bussed from Immokalee where Gaunt had a black camp called Bunker Hill and other camps for Mexican migrants. Tomato farming finally stopped after blight struck in 1965 and the land was sold to the federal park service to become part of Big Cypress National Preserve.

On the Trail, the intersection with Route 29 at Carnestown was rebuilt in 1950. The State Highway Patrol post and the Everglades Welcome Station (in its distinctive A-shaped wooden building) were built in 1965 on land leased from the Collier Development Corporation. The Everglades Area Chamber of Commerce, which operates the tourist information center, had been founded in 1956 and previously used space in City Hall.

A Brief History of the Everglades City Area

Further afield, Meece Ellis retired from road building and took over Royal Palm Hammock station (Routes 41 and 92), near the Collier Seminole State Park where he was instrumental in restoring the Bay City Walking Dredge that he had operated during the 1920's.

The isolation of Chokoloskee from the mainland had effects economically and socially. In the 1950's most of the inhabitants were strictly religious; women were frowned upon if they wore slacks instead of skirts and everyone was expected to attend church services. In 1955 there were 127 people from 37 families. The school boat took students past 4th grade to Everglades.

Courtesy of Florida State Archives, Photographic Collection
Boatyard on Chokoloskee in the 1950's.

As far back as 1935, a move was made to have a road built across the bay and there was talk of a WPA project. The county graded a roadbed (now Plantation Parkway) as far as Halfway Creek, locally known as "Mrs Smallwood's road" because of her activity in promoting the land bridge. The war intervened and it was not until 1954 that the project was continued with the revised route of the present causeway.

After the link was completed in 1956, Chokoloskee looked forward to an economic revival and trees were cleared in readiness for developers. Ted Smallwood's daughter Nancy Hancock and husband A. C. built the Blue Heron motel, marina, café, and campground near the Smallwood Store in 1956 and Ted's son Robert Daniel built another motel. A third, the Angler's

Rest (now part of Outdoor Resorts), was operated by Arvid Brown. Ted's daughter Thelma had taken over the Post Office in 1941, a position she held until 1973. The old wooden Church of God was replaced by a concrete structure.

THE NEW CITY

Barron Collier died in 1939. His businesses had suffered during the Depression and his expectations for the Town of Everglades were never fulfilled. One of the Trail workers paid him this tribute: "Mr. Collier was a great man. He did right by us all and did lots for this county"[1].

Of the next generation of Colliers, Samuel Carnes died in 1950 during a motor race at Watkins Glenn, NY, and Miles died in 1955 of polio. Barron, Jr, (who had a love of history), was left to run the Corporation with the help of N. A. Herren.

The Town of Everglades formally became a city when it received its charter in 1953. The Collier executives encouraged the new city to be independent. The first city mayor was Daniel McLeod, the county tax assessor and previously the town mayor.

The new City Council deliberated on issues that had previously been left to the Collier Development Corporation. Although the town council met in the Court House, the City decided to rent rooms in the old library building and first met there on April 13, 1954. City Hall was later moved to the Community Center, which the City had taken over from Collier in 1956 after pressure from the various groups and clubs that used it.

The Railway Light and Power Company, which originally served the streetcar and provided electricity to the community, was replaced in 1954 with a facility operated by Lee County Electricity Cooperative (LCEC) under a contract with the City.

---

[1] W.J. Rutledge quoted in Stone, *Dwellers of the Sawgrass and Sand, vol III*, p.58

Garbage collection was organized by the City. In 1957 the Council voted to increase the collector's wage from $1.00 to $1.10 an hour. Standardized garbage cans were required in 1962 for collection on Monday and Friday. The dump was on a piece of Collier ground north of the Trail, west of Route 29.

The school was replaced by a new building in 1959 and the City provided a sidewalk for the safety of the children. In 1956 the Baptist congregation moved the Methodist Church building from Jerome to a site across from the school and in 1964 permission was granted to build a small addition for a Sunday School.

The old market building near the Rod & Gun was offered by the Collier Development Company in 1956 to the City for use as a storage shed, if they would take it away. However, the Masons decided it would make a good lodge. After paying the City $1,000 in compensation, they moved the building to Storter Avenue and refurbished it. Just when it was ready, Hurricane Donna did so much damage that it took another two years to repair.

Hollywood came to the City of Everglades in 1957. Budd Schulberg (who wrote "On The Waterfront") chose the area for the setting of his script "Wind Across the Everglades" about plume hunters in 1905, based on the experiences and tales of Marco man Bud Kirk. The character Cottonmouth took its inspiration from a Pine Crest man who bought snakes from kids to sell in Miami. The film featured Christopher Plummer, Burl Ives, Gypsy Rose Lee plus locals like Totch Brown. The crew and cast took over the Rod & Gun Club and used the garage as a sound stage, thanks to cooperation from the Collier Corporation. City Hall (the old library building) was also a setting in the film, causing the council to proceed at its meeting without minutes. A donation was made by Schulberg to the Community Center.

Unfortunately, the heyday of the City was over, despite its recent incorporation. Collier County decided by referendum in 1959 to move the county seat to Naples, even though the City of Everglades was on the ballot. Dr. Snyder, the Mayor, initiated legal proceedings to prevent the move but lost. In 1962, the Council discussed proposing a new county, one that excluded Naples.

HURRICANE DONNA

The final justification for the county's departure was Hurricane Donna in 1960. The city was flooded to a depth of 8 feet and, although people took sanctuary in the upper story of the Court House, this building also suffered. Those who could followed the old custom of weathering out the storm in boats, sheltering in the highest reaches of the rivers and creeks. The City's disaster aid fund was some $34,000.

Courtesy of Florida State Archives, Photographic Collection
The Red Cross, in front of the jail, offered help after Donna.

Deaconess Bedell evacuated to Ochopee during the hurricane. The Glade Cross Mission was badly damaged and closed. The Deaconess moved to an ecclesiastic retirement home outside the area and died in 1969.

The Bank (which had money drying on the steps after Donna) moved in 1962 to Immokalee, despite protests from the City Council and Chamber of Commerce. The city was later served by a Bank Bus from First National of Naples and by a branch office of the First Bank of Marco which opened in City Hall in 1982. In 1996, the Fifth Third Bank pulled out of Everglades City.

A Brief History of the Everglades City Area

However, in 2009, Shamrock Bank of Florida opened a branch in special accommodation in the refurbished City Hall.

After the decision to move the county seat to Naples, the City Council proposed that the Court House be turned into the Collier County Historical Museum. Eventually, in 1963, the City accepted the Court House (which had been remodeled in 1957) for use as City Hall, with a proposal that some of the space be used as a museum. Other rooms were leased to private enterprises and the second floor was given over to the Community Center for meetings and teenage dances. By 1969 the library was open during office hours.

The council also approved a change of name to Everglades City. This required amending the city charter and passing a bill in the State Legislature, both of which were accomplished in 1965.

Deepening the channel to the Gulf, harbor improvements and the docks were among the early topics dealt with by the City Council. An ordinance of 1955 had attempted to control river traffic by restricting the speed to 4 m.p.h. within City limits. The river patrol could arrest "reckless" drivers. The penalty was a fine of $100 and/or 30 days in jail.

By 1960 the Harbor Act had passed the State Legislature, allowing for a channel (8 feet deep and 60 feet wide during low tide) as far as the 1.5 mile marker in the Barron River, up to the turning basin. In 1967 the public docks behind the school were leased to their occupants.

The ACL Rail Road operated until June 1956, with the station master living above the hall and ticket office. The City Council and the Chamber of Commerce protested about its closure, but ACL said there was not enough business. The tracks were removed in 1959. The historic station building has been preserved as a restaurant (now called the Seafood Depot).

However, the Tour Bus Line continued to make stops in the city. In 1964 the office was moved to the WinCar hardware store in the

Inn. In 1969 the service had dwindled from 7 buses a day to only 2, one in each direction, and caused concern because of the lack of freight delivery.

IMPROVEMENTS IN THE CITY

In 1962 a contractor was finally chosen to pave the roads, which the City periodically oiled to keep down the dust. Discussions had begun in 1956, with the Collier Corporation donating $5,000 towards a study. Although the City was responsible for ensuring the roadbed was in good order, individual residents paid for the paving of the street in front of their property.

The Beautification Committee tried to keep up the standards set by the Colliers. In 1961 the planting of trees and shrubs was begun in the road medians. Sprinklers and a fountain for the fish pond in one of the Broadway islands was proposed in 1963. After much protest about the nuisance caused by wandering beasts, a City ordinance of 1958 restricted the keeping of "grazing animals" (horses) to adequately large stalls with insect mesh.

The City had bought the lot west of the Court House in 1954 and eventually purchased the rest of the lots between there and the Bank building in 1968 after the Lions Club offered to help establish a public park. It was named in honor of Daniel McLeod who had served as Mayor of the Town and City for almost 35 years (January 1, 1925, until swearing in his successor Dr. Snyder on December 1, 1959). He died in September 1960, not long after his resignation. The McLeod monument on Circle, dedicated to the Mayor and his wife Lucy, was erected in 2008.

The Everglades National Park chose the City as its western gateway in 1953 and in 1961 was planning a boat basin and visitors' center to cater for up 1000 people per day. In 1965 the boat tour concession was awarded to Sammy Hamilton, Jr (who became Mayor of Everglades City).

The Rod & Gun added a new wing after being sold by the Collier Corporation in 1963. The Everglades Inn, which had been occupied by the Coast Guard during the war (as was the Rod & Gun), was converted into offices and apartments above stores on the ground floor. In 1968 the Captain's Table complex was developed after the City closed off the southern end of Collier Avenue and a small bit of Ixora Street. The owner built a sea wall on Lake Placid (which he donated to the City) as well as the docks and motel with pool. He also took over the Old Station Restaurant.

Other private developments were not so successful. There was a proposal in 1962 to build houses on Pleasure Island with a bridge crossing the river just south of the school (a plan originally sketched in on a 1931 map) and several developers applied for zoning permission for housing on the Point, at the mouth of the river near the airport.

Courtesy of Florida State Archives, Photographic Collection
The Atlantic Coast Line Rail Road depot in a photo from 1930 was converted into a restaurant after the train service stopped.

6 MODERN TIMES

The previous farming and logging industries have mostly disappeared because of the depletion of natural resources and the expansion of the Parks. Similarly, commercial fishing has become specialized, concentrating on stone crabs, after the net ban in 1995. Industry in the area is mainly service: to retirees and snowbirds, to short-term visitors (here for sports-fishing or nature study), and to administrators of the Parks. Many tourist businesses close during the summer when there are only weekenders from the large Florida cities here for the fishing or day-trippers, often European, on their way to the Park.

AROUND THE AREA

Some fifty years after the completion of the Trail, a second west-to-east road was built directly from Naples to Ft Lauderdale. Route 84 originally had only two lanes but was absorbed in the 1990's into the Interstate system and expanded to a four-lane toll road. Nicknamed "Alligator Alley", the canal parallel to I-75 does have alligators basking in the mud. Despite an interchange with Route 29 (after much pressure from local residents), the result of this new high-speed motorway is that casual spending by passing travelers has been drawn away from the area.

Collier's Tamiami Trail from Carnestown to Paolita is now mostly within one of the Parks, which have expanded, thanks partly to donations of land by the Collier interests. Big Cypress National Preserve and Fakahatchee Strand Preserve State Park were both established in 1974.

The little hose and pipe shed that was set up as a temporary Post Office after the Ochopee fire in 1953 is still operational and is "the smallest Post Office in the USA". Tourists often stop to take a photograph and have their post cards stamped from Ochopee.

A Brief History of the Everglades City Area

Courtesy of Florida State Archives, Photographic Collection
Ochopee Post Office.

Monroe Station was known as "The Tree with the Hole in It" because the telephone wires ran through a big tree at the front. It had been turned into Lord's Restaurant, which proclaimed "Marriages Performed Here". This landmark was bought by Big Cypress National Preserve and is closed.

However, the station did benefit from the Disney filming of "Gone Fishin" in 1996. The company paid local area businesses well for shooting on location and Totch Brown's song "Down the Everglades" was recorded by Willie Nelson.

Several miles further to the east is the Oasis Visitor Center, also part of Big Cypress. The administration of Big Cypress is headquartered in Ochopee in the former Golden Lion motel.

A Brief History of the Everglades City Area

In Copeland, the old logging road became Janes Scenic Drive through Fakahatchee Strand Preserve State Park. After Winford Janes died in 1962, the restaurant and store operated under new owners. The complex was sold in 2001 to Big Cypress National Preserve who tore down the buildings.

The Smallwood Store in Chokoloskee, which closed for business in 1982, received funds from the State and raised some itself when it held its first Seminole Indian Day in February 1991, with Marjory Stoneman Douglas (who was born in April, 1890) as its guest of honor. The Store is now a museum with a gift shop selling books of local interest.

IN THE CITY

The new causeway and the sell-off of Collier property encouraged the Smallwoods to expand their interests into Everglades City. By the 1980's they owned what is now Glades Haven opposite the National Park, a marina in DuPont (based in the old school house), and the land on the opposite side of the river, now Everglades Island Luxury Motorcoach Resort with its distinctive lighthouse club.

In the City center itself, a fire in 1987 changed the habits of a lifetime for many locals and the streetscape for future visitors. The Inn burnt down. Gone were Mama Dot's Malt Shop, the drug store, the sundries store and, unfortunately, files and records in the offices on the second floor. Only the WinCar hardware store survives, in a new location.

City Hall still serves the community. A branch of the Collier County public library offers books, videos, and Internet access. McLeod Park, maintained by the city, is the site for the annual Seafood Festival which draws thousands of visitors each February. The event began in 1973, the 50th anniversary of Collier's arrival, as the "Little Fish Fry", a means of raising money for McLeod park.

A Brief History of the Everglades City Area

In 1996 a completely new school complex costing $9.3 million was built, educating students from pre-K through 12th grade from the greater area (including some Indian children who travel from the reservation near the Dade County border). It is the only school in the state with all grades under one roof.

In the same year, the airport got new buildings, hangars and a sheriff's dwelling. Originally owned by the Collier Corporation, it was leased to the City in the early 1960's. The FAA approved it for landing but recommended a longer and wider runway which the City could not afford to build. It was eventually taken over by the County.

The old laundry building was used by the Women's Club, who bought it from the Collier Corporation in 1972. It received an historic marker in 1976. Some of the members were active in a movement to have permanent housing for a local museum and there was also concern about the structure of the laundry, which was in need of major repair. The Friends of the Museum of the Everglades was formed and raised money from various sources for the restoration. Exactly 70 years after the opening of the Trail, on April 26th, 1998, the Museum of the Everglades welcomed its first visitors.

The Everglades Community Church was restored in 2008 to its original wooden siding and received a State historic marker. Further work has refurbished the interior and enlarged the Louise Collier Jinkins Fellowship Hall.

Everglades City with its wealth of history was honored by having Deaconess Harriet Bedell and David Graham Copeland named as Great Floridians 2000 by the Department of State. Plaques for them are on the front of the Museum. The building itself was admitted to the exclusive list of the National Register of Historic Places in 2001. Other buildings on the Register are the old Bank, the Smallwood Store and Monroe Station.

APPENDIX I. CRACKERS

No one is really sure about the precise meaning and derivation of the word "cracker" which according to Webster's New World Dictionary (Second College Edition) is a derogatory term for "poor white". Its earlier meaning was "braggart, boaster".

Cracker was probably first used in South Georgia. It may refer to farmers cracking corn to make meal or to brew moonshine. Or, to cracking the hardtack biscuits that poor immigrants ate.

Alternatively, it describes the sound made by a whip, an implement used for herding cattle, driving oxen hitched to a plow, encouraging mules taking cotton to market, or disciplining slaves. In any case, it implied that a man of property was wielding it.

The whip was 1 inch in diameter and 14-16 feet long. It could also be used as a weapon in a fight with animals or other men and as a means of communication. The sound of the whip cracking carried long distances over open country and a code of whip cracks evolved: 1 for "hello", 2 for "I'm ok", 3 for "help".

Marjory Stoneman Douglas describes crackers as cattlemen who came south in 1842, living in Florida in primitive conditions. It has also been suggested that "cracker" is an English version of the Spanish for Quaker, also early settlers in the area.

Now crackers are natives described as having a "proud Florida back-country culture"[1] with a "love for the land, and God, and family that supersedes the values of fast-paced life"[2].

---

[1] Ste. Claire, *Cracker*, p.34

[2] Stein, *Florida Cracker Tales*, p.xx

APPENDIX II. PLACE NAMES

Barron River named after Barron Collier. Runs through Everglades City. Previously known as Potato Creek, Allen River, Everglade River, and Storter River.

Birdon Road (Route 41 near Ochopee) named after H.W. Bird and J. F. Jaudon who had tomato packing plant there in 1930's.

Carnestown (corner of Routes 41 & 29) named after Barron Collier's wife Juliet Carnes and their son Samuel Carnes Collier. Had warehouse and work camp during building of the Tamiami Trail. Now has Everglades Area Chamber of Commerce Welcome Center, Sheriff's sub-station, and garage with store.

Chevelier Bay named after company which tried to farm at Chatham Bend after Watson left in 1910.

Chokoloskee is Indian for "old home" or "old house" or "big house". Residential island at southern end of Route 29.

Comer Island (Comer Key) named after Governor of Georgia who visited there to fish from 1914 onwards.

Copeland (Route 29, north of Route 41) named after D. Graham Copeland, Collier's right-hand man and engineering supremo during the building of Tamiami Trail and Town of Everglades. Was farming and logging community.

Dan House Prairie (Route 41 at Port of the Islands) named after renowned rum-runner who farmed tomatoes there in 1930's.

Duck Rock was populous rookery for sea birds until the mangrove was destroyed by Hurricane Donna in 1960.

DuPont or **Port DuPont** named after DuPont family, friends of Barron Collier. On west side of Barron River in Everglades City, near Route 29 bridge. Was heavy engineering center during building of Tamiami Trail. Now predominately fishing port for crab boats.

A Brief History of the Everglades City Area

Everglades may be Indian for "river of grass" or may be a corruption of "river glades" or "ever glydes" meaning verdant. Everglades City originally called "Everglade" when Post Office was established in 1893, changed to "Everglades" by Collier.

Fakahatchee may be Indian for "forked water" or "muddy water". Fakahatchee Island has an old cemetery memoralizing early farmers and fishermen. Fakahatchee River leads to Weaver's Station from Fakahtchee Bay. Faka Union Canal leads to Port of the Islands. Fakahatchee Strand Preserve State Park is about 80,000 acres which includes Boardwalk at Weaver's Station on Route 41.

Halfway Creek is half way between Everglades and Chokoloskee. Was populous farming settlement at turn of century.

Jack Daniels Key possibly named after local fisherman and guide, one of Daniels family.

Janes Scenic Drive (off Route 29 at Copeland in Fakahatchee Strand Preserve State Park) named after Winford Janes, prominent in the area and a Collier County Commissioner. The road was the main cypress logging rail track.

Jerome (Route 29 north of Route 41) named after C. Jerome Jones who owned the pine logging operation and sawmill based in the area from 1940 to 1956.

Lopez River named after Lopez family, who also lived in Chokoloskee where there is a family cemetery.

Miles City (corner of Route 29 and Interstate 75) named after Barron Collier's son Miles. Was farming and later ranching settlement.

Monroe Station (Route 41 and Loop Road) was one of six Mounties stations along the Tamiami Trail. Loop Road leads into Monroe County to Pine Crest and Route 94, now all part of Big Cypress National Preserve.

Ochopee (Route 41, east of Route 29) is corruption of Ochoppee, Indian for "big farm". Was thriving tomato farming area. Now headquarters for Big Cypress National Preserve and has smallest Post Office in USA.

Panther Key (Goat Key) failed as goat farm when panthers ate them. Also known as **Gomez Key** after the old pirate who lived there.

Paolita (Route 41) named after D. Graham Copeland's daughter. Was one of six Mounties stations along the Tamiami Trail. Stone archway *(see page 72)* marking the Dade/Collier County border, knocked down 1958 during road widening.

Pavilion Key said to be named after the pirate Charles Gibbs who built a pavilion out of logs and palmetto for a wealthy Dutch girl he had captured and fallen in love with in 1820's.

Turner River named after Capt. Richard Turner who led expedition up river in 1857 during Indian wars and settled there in 1874.

Watson Place named after notorious outlaw E. J. Watson who farmed on Chatham Bend and was shot in Chokoloskee in 1910.

Weaver's Station or **Weaver's Camp** (Route 41 west of Route 29), originally known as Fakahatchee Station, was one of six Mounties stations along the Tamiami Trail, operated by S. M. Weaver. Was a convict camp. Now known as Big Cypress Bend, across the Trail from Fakahatchee Boardwalk.

Whiskey Creek had moonshine stills on its banks and was used for transporting whiskey to market.

SOURCES

The classic history of the area and further afield (Marco Island, Naples, Immokalee) is Tebeau's **Florida's Last Frontier** which was first published in 1957 and revised in 1966. Tebeau used Copeland's historical research papers under a grant from the University of Miami endowed by the sons of Barron Collier. The author also wrote a little book about Chokoloskee incorporating Ted Smallwood's early memoirs.

Fortunately, Maria Stone compiled collections of the tales told to her by people who lived during the building of the Trail and in the pioneering days of the southwest Florida. She published a number of books, many of which are available at Collier County public libraries.

For a first-hand account of life from the Depression up until the modern times, Totch Brown's memoirs **Totch** are interesting reading, especially his experiences trying to survive in the wilderness and his insider's view of smuggling. McKinney's brief biography for the *American Eagle* is included as an Appendix.

Rob Storter (1894-1987) sketched and wrote about his remembrances late in life. His works have been edited by his grand-daughter and published in the book **Crackers in the Glade**.

The Internet is invaluable for research. Most of the photographs in this book came from the Photographic Collection at the Florida State Archives (**www.floridamemory.com**). Many resources are available electronically through the academic inter-library system PALMM (**http://palmm.fcla.edu/**) and particularly interesting is the collection of digital documents in "Reclaiming the Everglades" (**http://everglades.fiu.edu/reclaim/**) which focuses on south Florida history from 1884 to 1934.

BOOKS

Akin, Edward N, **Flagler: Rockefeller Partner and Florida Baron**, 1991: University Press of Florida, Gainesville, FL (Florida railway pioneer)

Ames, Elizabeth Scott, **The Deaconess of the Everglades**, 1995: Cortland Press, Cortland, NY (biography of Deaconess Harriet Bedell)

Barnes, Jay, **Florida's Hurricane History**, 1998: University of North Carolina Press, Chapel Hill, NC (details of hurricanes since late 1800's to present)

Baum, Earl L, MD, **Early Naples and Collier County**, 1973: Collier County Historical Society, Naples, FL (memoirs, mostly about Naples)

Beater, Jack, **Tales of South Florida and the Ten Thousand Islands**, 1965: Jack Beater, Ft Myers, FL (stories about early settlers and places)

Beater, Jack, **True Tales of the Florida West Coast**, 1960: Jack Beater, Ft Myers, FL (stories about early settlers and places)

Brown, Loren G, **Totch: A Life in the Everglades**, 1993: University Press of Florida, Gainesville, FL (memoirs, living through the Depression, smuggling, includes McKinney reprints)

Carlin, Virginia, **I Remember Marco: A Tale of Two Villages**, 1999: Virginia Carlin Enterprises, Marco Island, FL (conversations with local people, some with Everglades connections)

Carter, W Hodding, **Stolen Water: Saving the Everglades from its Friends, Foes and Florida**, 2004: Atria Books, New York, NY (a journalist's often-cynical view of the Florida environment)

Cerulean, Susan, ed., **The Book of the Everglades**, 2002: Milkweed Editions, Minneapolis, MN (collection of articles, mostly about changes to the environment)

Collier County Museums, **Tamiami Trail: Florida's Modern Apian Way**, 2003: Collier County Museums, Naples, FL (booklet with photos issued for 75th anniversary of opening of Trail)

Copeland, D Graham, compiler, **Data Relative to Florida**, 1947: Everglades, FL (over 1000 typed pages of notes plus 64 pages of sources; copy presented by the author to the Florida State Library)

A Brief History of the Everglades City Area

Davis, Karen, **Public Faces – Private Lives: Women in South Florida, 1870s-1910s**, 1990: The Pickering Press, FL (ordinary life of pioneering women before the railroad changed the east coast)

Dimmock, A W, **Florida Enchantments**, 1915: A.W. Dimmock, Peekamose, NY (reports and photos of travels, many by canoe, through Ten-Thousand Islands, Big Cypress)

Douglas, Marjory Stoneman, **The Everglades: River of Grass**, 1947: Mockingbird Books, Marietta, GA (history and classic plea for Glades preservation)

Douglas, Marjory Stoneman (with John Rothchild), **Voice of the River, an Autobiography**, 1987: Pineapple Press, Sarasota, FL (interesting observations about her life in southern Florida from 1915)

Earl, Dean & Indi, eds., **Collier County Semi-Centenial**, 1973: Naples, FL (descriptions and photos of places in the County)

Everglades City School, **Prop Roots IV: Attractions of the Western Everglades**, 1987: Collier County Public Schools, Naples, FL (descriptions and photos of local restaurants and hotels)

Fritchey, John, **Everglades Journal**, 1992: Florida Heritage Press, Miami, FL (memoirs of living in Glades)

Friends of the Museum of the Everglades, **Historic Buildings around Everglades City: Walking Tours**, 2006: Friends of the Museum of the Everglades, Everglades City, FL (pictures and history of buildings)

Gannon, Michael, ed., **The New History of Florida**, 1996: University Press of Florida, Gainsville, FL (chapters in history written by invited contributors)

Griffin, Robert V, **Everglades Outlaws**, 2003: Xlibris Corporation, (memoirs about fishing and smuggling plus poems by the author)

Hartley, William & Ellen, **A Woman Set Apart**, 1963: Dodd, Mead & Co, New York, NY (biography of Deaconess Harriet Bedell)

Hoffman, Henry R, ed., **Collier County Heritage**, 1976: Heritage Publications, Naples, FL (articles about Trail, City, Marco, Naples, Hurricane Donna)

Lamme, Vernon, **More Florida Lore**, 1979: Star Publications, Boynton Beach, FL (stories about early settlers and places)

A Brief History of the Everglades City Area

Lynne, Erica, **Remembering Ochopee**, 1995: Wooten's Everglades Airboat Tours, Ochopee, FL (small history with map)

Magill, Inez, **From Ticks to Politics**, no date: published privately (memoirs of assistant county clerk who came to Everglades in 1951)

McIver, Stuart B, **Death in the Everglades: the Murder of Guy Bradley, America's First Martyr to Environmentalism**, 2003: University Press of Florida, Gainesville, FL (life at the turn of the 19th century in southern Florida and the effort to stop plume hunting)

McIver, Stuart B, **Touched by the Sun**, 2001: Pineapple Press, Sarasota, FL (stories about early Florida, including the filming of "Wind Across the Everglades" in 1957)

McIver, Stuart B, **True Tales of the Everglades**, 1989: Florida Flair Books, Miami, FL (stories about early settlers and places)

Morris, Allen, **Florida Place Names**, 1995: Pineapple Press, Sarasota, FL (dictionary of names with their origins)

Orlean, Susan, **The Orchid Thief**, 1998: Random House, New York, NY (story of author's search for orchids in Fakahatchee Strand, basis of Hollywood film "Adaptation")

Reynolds, Doris, **Peacocks Were Roasted, Mullet Was Fried**, 1993: Enterprise Publishing, Naples, FL (short biographies and recipies, some Everglades connections)

Rothra, Elizabeth Ogren, **Florida's Pioneer Naturalist: Life of Charles Torrey Simpson**, 1995: University Press of Florida, Gainsville, FL (biography with descriptions of countryside and wildlife)

Schulberg, Budd, **Across the Everglades**, 1958: Random House, New York, NY (script for movie with lengthy introduction)

Simmons, Glen and Laura Ogden, **Gladesmen**, 1998: University Press of Florida, Gainesville, FL (memoirs of living in Glades)

Simpson, Charles Torrey, **Florida Wild Life**, 1932: Macmillian, New York, NY (observations on wildlife, descriptions of southwest Florida in 1880's)

Ste Claire, Dana, **Cracker; The Cracker Culture in Florida History**, 1998: Museum of Arts and Sciences, Daytona Beach, FL (definitions and lifestyle of "crackers")

A Brief History of the Everglades City Area

Stein, Teresa E, **Florida Cracker Tales**, 1995: Placid Publications, Lake Placid, FL (definitions and lifestyle of "crackers")

Stone, Calvin R, **Forty Years in the Everglades**, 1979: Atlantic Publishing Co., Tabor City, NC (visitor to and hunter in Glades, 1930's to 1970's)

Stone, Maria, **Dwellers of the Sawgrass and Sand, vol II: Natives and Near Natives**, 1996: Stone Enterprises, Naples, FL (conversations with local people)

Stone, Maria, **Dwellers of the Sawgrass and Sand, vol III: Natives and Near Natives**, 1996: Stone Enterprises, Naples, FL (conversations with local people)

Stone, Maria, **Ochopee, The Story of the Smallest Post Office**, 1992: Stone Enterprises, Naples, FL (conversations with local people)

Stone, Maria, **The Tamiami Trail**, 1998: Stone Enterprises, Naples, FL (conversations with local people)

Stone, Maria, **We Also Came: Black People of Collier County**, 1992: Stone Enterprises, Naples, FL (conversations with local people)

Storter, Rob, with Betty Savidge Briggs, ed., **Crackers in the Glade**, 2000: University of Georgia Press, Athens, GA (memoirs with drawings)

Storter, Robert L, **Seventy-seven Years in Everglades, Chokoloskee, Naples**, 1972: published privately, (memoirs, mostly included in **Crackers in the Glades**)

Tebeau, Charlton W, **Florida's Last Frontier: The History of Collier County**, 1966: University of Miami Press, Miami, FL (classic history from first Indians to 1960's)

Tebeau, Charlton W, **Man in the Everglades**, 1968: University of Miami Press, Coral Gables, FL (history of Indians and settlers in the National Park, including Ten-Thousand Islands)

Tebeau, Charlton W, **Story of Chokoloskee Bay Country**, 1976: Florida Flair Books, Miami, FL (history, includes reprint of Smallwood memoirs)

Turner, Gregg M, **Railroads of Southwest Florida**, 1999: Arcadia Publishing, Charleston, SC (part of "Images of America" series, good photographs, mentions logging railroads as well as Atlantic Coast Line and Seaboard Coast Line)

A Brief History of the Everglades City Area

PERIODICALS

"Haunting Heart of the Everglades", Andrew H Brown, *National Geographic*, Washington, DC, Feb 1948 (report of trip to Town of Everglades and through Glades)

"Star Struck in the Glades", Stuart McIver, *Sun Sentinel*, Ft Lauderdale, FL, July 28, 1996 (making of the film "Wind Across the Everglades")

"The Florida Story Begins with Audubon Wardens", Leslie Kemp Poole, *Florida Naturalist*, Audubon of Florida, Miami, FL, Summer 2000 (plume hunters, killing of Guy Bradley)

"UF's First Gators", Carl van Ness, *TODAY, Alumni Assoc. Magazine*, University of Florida, Gainsville, FL, Sept, 1960 (about Neil Storter and the football team)

Everglades Echo, Tuff Publications, Naples, FL (weekly newspaper)

Naples Daily News (formerly *Collier County News*), Naples, FL, 1923 to present (on microfilm at Collier County Public Library)

Neapolitan Magazine Centennial Issue, Naples, FL, vol. IX, no. 1, 1985 (articles about the Trail, Lucy Storter, Juan Gomez)

South Florida History, Historical Association of Southern Florida, Miami, FL (articles of general interest)

Tequesta, Journal of the Historical Association of Southern Florida, Miami, FL (learned articles about historical topics)

ORIGINAL SOURCES

Everglades Seafood Festival, Organized Fishermen of Florida, Everglades City, FL, 1995 (program with historical notes)

Gallery Guide to Exhibition, "Everglade to Everglades City, 1989-1999", Museum of the Everglades, Everglades City, FL, 1999 (description of historic photos on display)

letter, D Graham Copeland, Everglades, FL, 3/10/1945 (news about local soldiers during WWII, reproduced by WinCar Hardware, 7/4/2004)

letter, N A Herren, Naples, FL, 3/15/2001 (history and memoirs of early Collier company)

Minute Books, City Council, Everglades City, FL, 1953-69

A Brief History of the Everglades City Area

Minute Books, Board of County Commissioners, Collier County, 1923 to present (on microfilm at County offices)

recollections, M G Iles, Everglades City, FL, 1998 (memoirs 1954, additions 1998)

Scrap Books, Women's Club, Everglades City, Fl, 1963-84 (include cuttings from newspapers)

Storytellers, Kerrie Chobot, recorder, Museum of the Everglades, Everglades City, FL, April 28, 2001 (memoirs told at the Museum's birthday party)

Storter Collection, Collier County Museums, Naples, FL (sketches and stories by Rob Storter, 1894-1987)

FICTION

Ayres, E C, **Night of the Panther**, 1997: St Martin's Press, New York, NY (detective story set in the Big Cypress, deals with the conflict among different interest groups)

Johnson, Franklyn A, **Santori: Island of Evil**, 1999: Francobollo Press, Bonita Springs, FL (fanciful suspense novel by former resident)

Kaserman, James, **Gasparilla: Pirate Genius**, Pirate Publishing International, Fort Myers, FL (historical novel)

Lewbart, Greg, **Pavilion Key, Isle of Buried Treasure**, 2000: Krieger Publishing, Malabar, FL (historical novel)

MacDonald, John D, **Condominium**, 1977: Random House, New York, NY (a cautionary novel by a masterful author about development on the Gulf Coast, not in the Travis McGee series)

Mattheissen, Peter, **Bone by Bone**, 1999: Random House, New York, NY

Mattheissen, Peter, **Killing Mister Watson**, 1990: Random House, New York, NY (classic historical novel about the area)

Mattheissen, Peter, **Lost Man's River**, 1997: Random House, New York, NY

White, Randy Wayne, **The Man Who Invented Florida**, 1993: St Martin's Press, New York, NY (amusing story of fictional village with magical elixir of life)

Courtesy of Florida State Archives, Photographic Collection

The Tamiami Trial at the Collier/Dade county border in 1928. Note that, although the road is higher than the surrounding land, it is not paved. The building of the Trail resulted in major changes, both good and bad, to "Florida's Last Frontier". It made the area available to motor vehicles but stopped the flow of water through the Glades from north to south. The arch was torn down when the road was widened in 1958.

INDEX

A
airport, 60
Allen, William Smith, 9, 10
Alligator Alley, 57
Atlantic Coast Line (ACL) Rail Road, 8, 11, 25, 33, 37, 54
Ayers, Chris and Lois, 34

B
bank, 34, 35, 53, 55, 60
Barfield, Mrs Tommie (Marco Island), 24
Barron River, 9, 21, 24, 25, 26, 31, 33, 35, 37, 44, 54, 56, 59
    Allen River, 9, 10, 11, 12, 14, 15, 17, 20, 24
    Everglade River, 8, 9
    Potato Creek, 9
    Storter River, 9
    traffic control, 54
Baum, Earl L. (historian), 45
Bedell, Deaconess Harriet, 36, 46, 53, 60
Belle Meade, 29
Bird, H.W., 39
Birdon, 39, 49
Black, Ed, 31
Boggess, Charles, 12
Bradley, Guy (Audubon warden), 16
Broward, Napoleon Bonaparte (Governor), 47
Brown family, 7, 10, 15, 18, 19, 51
Brown, Totch, 19, 43, 45, 52, 58
Bruner, George, 19

C
C. J. Jones Company, 42
Capone, Al, 45
Carnestown, 24, 25, 26, 39, 49, 57
Chamber of Commerce, 49, 53, 54
Chatham River, 8, 11, 18
Chevelier Corporation, 18
Chokoloskee, 8, 9, 10, 11, 13, 14, 15, 16, 18, 19, 37, 41, 43, 44, 45, 46, 50
    "big house", 10
    "old home", 10
    "old house", 10
    causeway, 50, 59
church, 45
    Chokoloskee, 50, 51
    DuPont, 25, 35
    Everglade, 14
    Everglades, 25, 34, 35, 41
    Everglades City, 52
    Halfway Creek, 12, 15
    Ochopee, 41
City Hall, 49, 51, 52, 53, 54, 59
Civil War, 7, 9, 11
Clay, William, 10
Collier Company, 24, 28, 29, 31, 33, 34, 36, 37, 41, 43, 46, 49, 51, 52, 55, 57, 59, 60
Collier County, 7, 21, 26, 28, 37, 52, 54, 59
Collier, Barron Gift, 20, 21, 24, 25, 27, 28, 29, 31, 33, 34, 35, 37, 40, 51, 57
Collier, Barron, Jr (son), 25, 33, 51

Collier, Juliet Carnes (wife), 21, 25, 35
Collier, Miles (son), 25, 33, 43, 46, 51
Collier, Samuel Carnes (son), 25, 33, 51
Collier, W.D. (Capt Bill, son of W.T.), 9, 16
Collier, W.T. (Marco Island), 9
Community Center, 34, 35, 37, 51, 52, 54
Copeland, David Graham, 24, 26, 29, 31, 33, 37, 60
Copeland, town, 41, 42, 49, 59
Court House, 25, 35, 37, 51, 53, 54, 55

D

Dade County, 23, 24, 28, 29, 47, 48, 60
Deep Lake, 20, 21, 23, 24, 25, 41
Depression, 29, 39, 43, 51
Dickey, E.P., 23
Disney ("Gone Fishin"), 58
Dixie, I., 23
Douglas, Marjory Stoneman, 48, 59
dredge, 16, 19, 24, 26, 43, 47
  Barcarmil, 25
  Bay City Walking Dredge, 26, 50
DuPont (Port DuPont), 10, 20, 25, 26, 33, 35, 59

E

Echols, Ralph, 34
Ellis, Meece, 26, 50
Everglades City, 9, 52, 54, 55, 59, 60
  city charter 1953, 51, 54

Everglade, 12, 13, 14, 15, 16, 17, 19, 20, 23, 24, 44
  name change, 54
  Town of Everglades, 18, 21, 25, 26, 27, 28, 29, 31, 36, 37, 41, 43, 44, 46, 50, 51
Everglades Inn, 33, 34, 35, 38, 55, 59

F

Fakahatchee, 29, 41
farming, 8, 12, 13, 39, 41, 43, 46, 57
  avocados, 8, 15, 41
  bananas, 8, 9
  citrus fruit, 8, 21, 23
  sugar cane, 8, 9, 10, 12, 18, 43, 45
  tomatoes, 8, 9, 10, 12, 39, 40, 41, 43, 44, 49
fishing, 8, 12, 13, 15, 19, 20, 38, 39, 43, 46, 57
  clamming, 8, 9, 15, 16
  mullet, 8, 43
  oyster, 8
  shrimp, 57
Flagler, Henry (Rail Roads), 9
Fort Myers, 7, 8, 11, 15, 19, 20, 23, 33

G

Gatewood, Rev. George, 12, 14
Gators (football team), 17
Gaunt, James, 36, 39, 40, 41, 47, 49
Glade Cross Mission, 36, 53
Glades, 17, 24, 26, 44, 47
  draining, 47
Gomez, Juan, 11, 13, 14
Griffin, Sidney, 19

H

Halfway Creek, 8, 10, 12, 15, 50
Hamilton, Sammy, Jr (Mayor), 55
Hancock, Nancy Smallwood, 50
Harris, Dr, 12, 15
Hendry County, 21
Herren, N.A., 49, 51
Holzman, Walter, 33
hospital, 25, 35
House family, 7, 13, 15, 18
House, Dan, 41
hunting, 8, 11, 12, 15, 28, 43, 44, 46, 47
  alligators, 8, 11, 13
  deer, 8, 29, 47
  deer, tick eradication, 47
  frogs, 47
  plume hunting, 8, 10, 16, 44, 52
  raccoons, 8, 15, 48
  turkeys, 8, 29, 37
hurricane
  1873, 10
  1910, 17, 18
  1926, 19, 27, 39, 41
  1960 (Donna), 52, 53
hurricanes, 36
Hutto, Bill (Chief of Police), 45

I

Immokalee, 8, 25, 33, 35, 36, 40, 42, 49, 53
Indians, 7, 9, 12, 14, 16, 23, 24, 27, 36, 37, 42, 43, 48, 60
Ivey House (B&B), 35
Ivey, Earl, 26, 35

J

Janes, J.B., 39, 41
Janes, Wayne, 41
Janes, Winford, 41, 59
Jaudon, J.F. (Frank), 18, 23, 24, 29, 39
Jerome, 42, 49, 52
Jetport, 48

K

Key West, 8, 9, 10, 12, 13, 25, 41, 45
Kirk, Bud ("Wind Across the Everglades"), 52

L

Lake Placid, 25, 56
Langford, Walter, 20
laundry, 25, 34, 60
Lee County, 8, 15, 21
Lee Tidewater Cypress Company, 42
logging, 25, 28, 41, 42, 43, 48, 57, 59
Loop Road, 8, 28, 45, 47, 49
Lopez, Gregorio, 16

M

Manhattan Mercantile, 29, 33, 35
Marco Island, 8, 13, 16, 24, 27, 33, 36, 41, 45, 49, 52, 53
McKinney, G.C., 11, 13, 14, 17, 18, 19
McLeod Park, 55, 59
McLeod, Daniel (Mayor), 51, 55
medical care, 8, 17, 27, 35, 42
Miami, 9, 13, 23, 27, 28, 29, 35, 36, 45, 48, 52
Miles City, 43
Monroe County, 8, 26, 45, 48
Monroe Station, 28, 29, 44, 47, 58, 60
moonshine, 11, 43
  "jugged lightning", 44

"low bush lightning", 44
"white mule", 44
Mounties (Southwest Mounted Patrol), 29, 35

N
Naples, 8, 23, 40, 42, 43, 45, 49, 52, 53, 54, 57

O
Ochopee, 29, 36, 39, 40, 46, 49, 53, 57, 59
    "big farm", 39
    "big field", 39
Okeechobee, 7, 47

P
Panther Key, 11, 13, 14
Paolita, 29, 57
Parks, 57
    Big Cypress National Preserve, 49, 58, 59
    Collier Seminole State Park, 26, 29, 50
    Everglades National Park, 46, 55
    Fakahatchee Strand State Preserve, 59
Pavilion Key, 11, 16
Perry, Anna Mae ("Mother"), 42
Pine Crest, 28, 45, 47, 52
pirates, 7, 11, 13
Plantation Island, 50
Port of the Islands, 41
Possum Key, 43
Post Office, 11
    Chokoloskee, 13, 51
    Copeland, 59
    Everglade, 14
    Everglades, 25, 33
    Ochopee, 40, 49, 58

Prohibition, 43, 44

R
ranching, 43, 47
Roach, John, 20
Rod & Gun, 10, 33, 34, 35, 37, 38, 46, 52, 55
Royal Palm, 29, 50

S
Sand Fly Island, 8, 9, 11, 12
Santini family, 11, 13
school
    Chokoloskee, 14
    Copeland, 42
    DuPont, 25, 35, 59
    Everglade, 14, 17, 19
    Everglades, 25, 35, 38, 41, 43
    Everglades City, 52, 54, 56, 60
    Immokalee, 42
Schulberg, Budd ("Wind Across the Everglades"), 52
Schultz, Dutch (Chicago Purple Gang), 45
Seminole Lodge, 35
Senghaas, Claus ("Snooky"), 33, 38
Shands survey (1902), 15
Short, Henry, 18
Simpson, Charles Torrey (naturalist), 23
Smallwood family, 59
Smallwood Store, 16, 18, 19, 37, 50, 59, 60
Smallwood, C.S.(Ted), 13, 15, 16, 17, 19
Smallwood, Mamie (nee House), 13, 50
Smallwood, Robert Daniel (son), 50

A Brief History of the Everglades City Area

Smallwood, Thelma (daughter), 51
smuggling
 aliens, 45
 bootlegging, 44, 45
 marijuana ("pot-hauling"), 45
 sugar, 45
Snyder, Dr. K. (Mayor), 52, 55
Storter family, 7
Storter, George, Jr, 10, 12, 14, 15, 17, 21, 24, 44
Storter, George, Sr, 10, 12
Storter, Neil (son of George, Jr), 17
Storter, R.B. (Bembery), 10, 12, 13, 14, 35
Storter, Rob (son of Bembery), 14, 15, 19
streetcar, 20, 25, 33, 51
swamp buggy, 29, 47
Swycover, August, 10

T

Tamiami Trail, 21, 23, 24, 25, 26, 27, 28, 29, 39, 40, 41, 43, 49, 51, 52, 57, 60
Tampa, 23, 25, 27
Ten-Thousand Islands, 7, 8, 11, 13, 43, 45
Todd (schoolteacher), 14
Trailblazers, 24
Trailways Bus Line, 27, 28, 49, 54
Truman, Harry S. (President), 46
Turner River, 8, 9, 12, 13, 15, 17, 29
Turner, Capt Richard, 9, 11

U

Useppa Island, 20, 34

V

Von Pfister, Capt, 11

W

Watson, E.J., 11, 18
Webb, Alfred, 41
Weeks, John, 7, 9, 11, 16
Weeks, Madison, 9, 10
Wiggins, Joe, 11
Wild Hog Roast, 47
Wilkerson, Frank, 44

Courtesy of Florida State Archives, Photographic Collection

Collier County Court House around 1953. The building was completed in 1928, at a cost of less than $25,000. It has been added to several times since then. After the county seat moved to East Naples in 1962, it became Everglades City Hall. It was damaged by Hurricane Wilma in October 2005 but has been completely restored and is used daily for City and County business. The Everglades Society for Historic Preservation has an office and Historical Library on the second floor.

NOTES

NOTES